*In celebration of Maryland's 350th Anniversary and
The Walters Art Gallery Golden Jubilee,
marking the 50th Anniversary of its opening as a public museum,
The Walters Art Gallery presents*

The Taste of Maryland

Art Collecting in Maryland 1800–1934

*An exhibition at The Walters Art Gallery, Baltimore
18 May–19 August, 1984*

Contributing Authors

G.A.	Gina Alexander, Intern, The Walters Art Gallery
L.H.A.	Leopoldine H. Arz, Registrar, The Walters Art Gallery
B.B.	Bernard Barryte, Curatorial Consultant, The Walters Art Gallery
D.M.B.	Diana M. Buitron, Curator of Greek and Roman Art, The Walters Art Gallery
J.V.C.	Jeanny Vorys Canby, Curator of Ancient Near Eastern and Egyptian Art, The Walters Art Gallery
S.T.C.	Stiles Tuttle Colwill, Chief Curator/Curator of Paintings, The Maryland Historical Society
W.R.J.	William R. Johnston, Associate Director/Curator of 18th- and 19th-Century Art, The Walters Art Gallery
L.M.C.R.	Lilian M. C. Randall, Curator of Manuscripts and Rare Books, The Walters Art Gallery
R.H.R.	Richard H. Randall, Jr., Curator of Medieval Art, Arms and Armor, The Walters Art Gallery
S.G.T.	Susan G. Tripp, Director, University Collections, The Johns Hopkins University
E.R.W.	Ellen Reeder Williams, Assistant Professor, The George Washington University

Cover illustration:
Jean-Léon Gérôme, *The Duel After the Masquerade* (no.94)

©1984 by The Trustees of The Walters Art Gallery,
600 North Charles Street,
Baltimore, Maryland 21201, U.S.A.
All rights reserved

Library of Congress no.84-050714

ISBN 0-911886-28-1

Printed in the United States of America

Project Coordinator: William R. Johnston
Assistant Project Coordinator: Bernard Barryte
Editor: Carol Strohecker
Assistant Editor: Charlotte M. Zinser
Editorial Assistance: Muriel L. Toppan
        Barbara A. Rothermel
Photography for The Walters Art Gallery: Susan E. Tobin
Design and Production Coordination: Carol Strohecker
Typesetting: The TypeWorks
        Keyboarding—Charlotte M. Zinser
        Interpretation—Bruce Lenes
        Type for cover—Alpha Graphics
Art Preparation: John Cole
        Barry Miller
Printing: Collins Lithographing & Printing Co.

Produced entirely in Baltimore, Maryland

Contents

In general, the collectors are arranged in this catalogue chronologically, by date of birth (with the exception of the Walters father and son, who are included at the end of the book). The names are cited at the bottom of each page containing descriptions of the works collected. To further facilitate the location of an individual collector and the corresponding works of art, however, the names are listed here alphabetically.

Preface

The Taste of Maryland commemorates two anniversaries: the 350th of the founding of the State of Maryland and the 50th of The Walters Art Gallery as a public museum. The selection of materials is intended to present a representative cross section of the history of taste in Maryland through a sampling of collections varying in scope and content. In date, the exhibition ranges from the end of the eighteenth century through 1934, the year The Walters opened as a public institution. Geographically, the show spans the state, bringing to light a wealth of material in a variety of media, including antiquities, medieval manuscripts, and decorative arts, in addition to paintings and sculpture.

The exhibition opens propitiously with a selection of works that once belonged to Robert Gilmor, Jr., one of the country's earliest collectors and patrons of the arts, whose aspiration to bequeath his holdings to a public institution failed to materialize because of financial setbacks experienced late in life. The development of interest in the fine arts in Maryland is then traced through a survey of some of the most notable nineteenth-century collections. Deplorably, in some instances, particularly those involving collectors outside Baltimore, documentation has remained scanty or nonexistent. Also highlighted in the show are several early twentieth-century collectors who, through their taste, perspicacity, and courage, set the course still followed by our public institutions today. It is to them that *The Taste of Maryland,* an exhibition affirming Maryland's artistic patrimony, is dedicated.

The Walters extends its gratitude to the individual and institutional lenders who have made this exhibition possible. Included among them are The Arnot Art Museum, Elmira; The Baltimore Museum of Art, Baltimore; The Corcoran Gallery of Art, Washington, DC; The Evergreen House Foundation, Baltimore; Goucher College, Towson; The Johns Hopkins University, Baltimore: Archaeological Museum, The Milton S. Eisenhower Library, and The Evergreen House; The Johns Hopkins Hospital, Baltimore; The John G. Johnson Collection, Philadelphia; The Library of Congress, Washington, DC; The Maryland Historical Society, Baltimore; The Maryland Institute, College of Art, Baltimore; The Memorial Art Gallery of The University of Rochester, Rochester; Mount Saint Mary's College, Special Collections/Archives House, Emmitsburg; The Museum of Fine Arts, Boston; The Peabody Institute of The City of Baltimore; Princeton University, Princeton, The Art Museum and The Library; and several private collectors. A special debt is due to colleagues who shared their knowledge with us: Gerald M. Ackerman, Art Department, Pomona College; James H. Cheevers, Curator, United States Naval Academy; William Voss Elder III, Curator of Decorative Arts, The Baltimore Museum of Art; Kelly Fitzpatrick, Special Collections/Archives House, Mount Saint Mary's College; Ann Gwyn, Assistant Library Director for Special Collections, The Milton S. Eisenhower Library, The Johns Hopkins University; Kathleen Hunt, Librarian for the Rosenwald Collection, Rare Book and Special Collections Division, The Library of Congress; Sona K. Johnston, Associate Curator for Paintings and Sculpture, The Baltimore Museum of Art; Carole Lindsley, Exhibitions Coordinator, Goucher College; William Matheson, Chief, Rare Book and Special Collections Division, The Library of Congress; Susan G. Pearl, History Division, The Maryland National Capital Park and Planning Commission; John Pollini, Assistant Professor of Classical Art and Archaeology and Curator of The Johns Hopkins University Archaeological Museum; Jean F. Preston, Curator of Manuscripts, Princeton University Library; Brenda Richardson, Assistant Director for Art, Curator of Paintings and Sculpture, The Baltimore Museum of Art; and Gregory Weidman, Curator of Furniture, The Maryland Historical Society. The success of *The Taste of Maryland* and its catalogue rests upon the expertise and creativity of the Gallery's curators and of the contributors from our sister Baltimore institutions. Finally, we wish to express our appreciation to the entire Walters staff, whose cooperation was essential for the realization of this exhibition.

Robert P. Bergman
Director, The Walters Art Gallery

Introduction

In 1766, the Provincial Assembly resolved to erect in Annapolis a marble statue dedicated to William Pitt. According to J. Thomas Scharf, chronicler of early Maryland, this statue represented the first documented indication of a taste for art in the state.[1] Ample evidence suggests, however, that during the eighteenth century, the wealthy residents of eastern and southern Maryland enjoyed a gracious style of living, much as did their counterparts in Tidewater Virginia. Writing in Annapolis on the eve of the Revolution, an English visitor, William Eddis, commented on the "many pleasant villas" in the town's vicinity, the speedy importation of fashions from the mother country, and "the natural ease and elegance" of the inhabitants.[2] Though art collecting was not pursued at this time, many houses were well furnished and some were adorned with portraits by artists such as Justus Engelhart Kühn, Gustavus and John Hesselius, John Wollaston, and Charles Willson Peale, who practiced in the area.[3] Indifference, preoccupation with more pressing needs, and antipathy for the fine arts as manifestations of Old World "despotism" and "superstition" might all have contributed to the absence of a more zealous pursuit of the fine arts.[4]

The earliest significant art collection to figure, however briefly, in Maryland's cultural life was imported from abroad. In 1794, Henri-Joseph, Baron de Stier, and his wife, a great-granddaughter of Peter Paul Rubens, fleeing the French revolutionaries in Belgium, came to this country bringing their family and their collection of paintings.[5] At first, the Stiers resided in Annapolis, but in 1802 they built a manor house, "Riversdale," in Prince Georges County, six miles outside Washington, DC.[6] Modeled after the Château du Mick, a Stier residence near Antwerp, "Riversdale" was intended to feature a painting room that would provide an "unequalled luxury in America for several centuries."[7] In 1803, the Stiers returned to Belgium, leaving the manor house to their daughter, Rosalie Eugenie, who had married George Calvert, a descendant of Maryland's Lords Proprietors. The family collection of paintings, numbering sixty-three works by Flemish, Dutch, and Italian artists, remained stored in crates, except for an airing that was witnessed by Gilbert Stuart.[8] Prior to being returned to Belgium in 1816, the pictures were exhibited for several days to guests from Washington.

Early in the nineteenth century, Baltimore emerged as the commercial, and eventually as the cultural center of the state. Its role as a port, as well as its strategic location at the hub of a vast transportation network that eventually included canals, turnpikes, and railroads serving the hinterlands, led to Baltimore's phenomenal growth and its displacement of Boston as the nation's third largest city in the 1830s.

Initially, cultural life was overshadowed by business pursuits. A severe critic of the city, Elizabeth Patterson Bonaparte, described the local men as "merchants" lacking a single idea "beyond their counting-houses,"[9] and the artist, Rembrandt Peale, echoed this opinion, writing that "liberal views and the purposes of science" were being sacrificed here to "the sordid calculations of shortsighted commercial avarice."[10] In such an environment, institutions promoting the visual arts—athenaeums, academies, and historical societies—evolved more slowly than in the cities to the north.[11] An exception was The Baltimore Museum and Gallery of Paintings, established in 1814 by Rembrandt Peale, in a building on Holliday Street, which was expressly designed by Robert Cary Long, Sr.[12] Intended to serve as "an elegant rendezvous of taste, curiosity and leisure," the Museum presented a mixed fare: a gallery of portraits of national heroes, exhibits of important pictures, such as Rembrandt Peale's *Court of Death*, John Vanderlyn's *Ariadne Asleep on the Island of Naxos*, and Benjamin West's *Musidora*, as well as quasi-scientific displays and natural curios, including the bones of a mastodon, Baltimore's first Egyptian mummy, and the tattooed head of a New Zealand chief. Rembrandt's brother, Rubens Peale, assumed management of the institution in 1822, introducing the first in a sequence of five annual exhibitions of paintings and various other works of art drawn from the Peale family holdings and from various local collections. The surviving catalogues for the years 1823 and 1825 both list more than two hundred works, including portraits by contemporary American artists as well as pictures attributed to Backhuysen, Leonardo da Vinci, Wouvermans, Teniers, Canaletti [sic], and Corregio [sic]. Despite his efforts, the Museum faltered, and in 1830 Rubens sold the building and withdrew to Philadelphia.

Other short-lived institutions included a Baltimore Athenaeum, intended to promote literature, the arts, and scholarship, which opened in 1824 but disappeared following a fire in the 1830s.[13] In 1838, several prominent citizens, headed by the jurist William F. Frick, established The Maryland Academy of Fine Arts, which promised to be a place of "rational and intellectual enjoyment," an addition of "immense moral value," and a source of "honor and dignity" for the city.[14] Appointments of professors of art, sculpture, anatomy, chemistry, architecture, and engraving were announced and a date was set that September for the first exhibition. The prevailing recession apparently took its toll, for the Academy ceased to be mentioned in the press. Equally ephemeral was the Maryland Art Association, composed of artists and amateurs who united briefly in 1847 to promote the knowledge and practice of the fine arts.[15]

Fortunately, encouragement of the arts was a role assumed by The Maryland Historical Society at its outset in 1844.[16] Formed that year by a number of Baltimoreans, headed by Brantz Mayer, the organization received its first accommodations three years later, when the Athenaeum Building was erected by public subscription and presented to the Society to share with two older library associations, the Library Company of Baltimore (started in the 1790s) and the Mercantile Library Association (established in 1839). The first in a number of yearly loan exhibitions was held by the Society in the third-floor galleries of the Athenaeum Building in 1847. The catalogues published on this and subsequent occasions listed impressive arrays of Old Master paintings, many of unquestionably optimistic attribution, as well as works by regional artists borrowed from local collectors.[17]

Although Baltimore in the first half of the nineteenth century lagged in the evolution of cultural institutions, it yielded a number of distinguished collectors. Preeminent among them was Robert Gilmor, Jr., the son of a wealthy merchant of Scottish origin.[18] While his father represented American business interests abroad in the 1780s, young Gilmor was educated in Amsterdam and in Marseilles. From 1799 to 1801, he undertook a Grand Tour of the Continent and in 1817/18, he made another trip to Europe. Benefiting from this foreign travel, Gilmor brought to his collecting a degree of sophistication unique in contemporary America. His interests were all-encompassing. Among the sources of his impressive acquisitions of paintings by Dutch and Italian Old Masters were the dealers, Michael Paff and P. Flandin in New York, and a number of agents abroad, among them Chevalier Aportool, director of the Royal Museum, Amsterdam. Robert Gilmor also patronized American artists, helping to promote the careers of several—notably Thomas Cole, Horatio Greenough, and Thomas Doughty. Gilmor also formed an important library which included several medieval manuscripts—among them a Book of Hours by the Rohan Master and an English Bible (no. 49). He was equally committed to other fields, such as autographs, engravings, drawings, and minerals. The extent of his interest in antiquities was not recorded, but Gilmor was known to have bought some ancient fragments in Nîmes in 1800, and his portrait by W. J. Hubard shows the collector standing beside a red-figure amphora and a *kylix* (no. 12). Although Gilmor's range of interests may not have been exceptional by international standards, it was unquestionably impressive in America, as is borne out in Horatio Greenough's account of his stay at "Beech Hill," the Gilmor residence to the west of the city:

> I work in Mr. Gilmore's [sic] library, finished in Gothic style receiving the light through a painted window. The air of art is all around me. Exquisite pictures of Italian and Flemish masters fill the compartments between the bookcases; books of prints load the side tables; little antique bronzes, heads, and medals crowd each other on the mantle-piece [sic].[19]

A bizarre episode in the history of Maryland collecting is presented by Colonel Mendes Cohen, a Baltimore banker and veteran of the Battle of Fort McHenry, who retired from business in 1829 and embarked on a six-year tour of Europe and the eastern Mediterranean. In 1832, the stalwart Baltimorean sailed up the Nile as far as Wady Halfa, conveying a homemade American flag, the first to be seen in the region. As a collector, Mendes Cohen assembled a number of Egyptian artifacts and a coin collection numbering twenty-four hundred items (see nos. 15–19).[20]

A more characteristic collector for his time was Dr. Thomas Edmondson, Jr., who is remembered as a patron of Ernst Georg Fischer, a genre painter from Coburg, Germany, active in Maryland during the early 1850s; of Nicolino Calyo, a Neapolitan view painter who visited Baltimore in 1834; and of the local artists Alfred J. Miller, Richard Caton Woodville, and Hugh Newell. Inheriting wealth at an early age, Edmondson never practiced medicine, his field of study at the University of Maryland, but devoted himself to such pursuits as horticulture and musical instruments, as well as art. Many of his exotic plants were eventually acquired by Thomas Winans for his Baltimore mansion, "Alexandroffsky," and the fate of Edmondson's violin collection, said to have included two Stradivari and a Guarnerius, remains unknown.[21] Edmondson participated in the meetings of the Gallery Committee of The Maryland Historical Society, lending generously to the yearly exhibitions. At the sixth exhibition, held in 1858, 105 works borrowed from his estate were shown, revealing that his interests were

Figure 1. *"Needwood," or "Needwood Forest," the late eighteenth-century house near Burkittsville, Frederick County, was built for Thomas Sim Lee, who twice was governor of Maryland.*

broader than previously thought and that he had even acquired a *Winter Piece (Peasants' Dancing)* attributed to Brueghel, a *Poultry Yard* by M. Hondecoeter, two mythological subjects by Daniel Seghers, and a typhoon scene by an unidentified Chinese artist.

Elsewhere in Maryland, there may have been occasional assemblages of paintings, such as the Lee family's holdings of Renaissance and Baroque paintings at "Needwood" in Frederick County (fig. 1). There were not yet, however, urban centers in the state capable of sustaining significant activity in the fine arts. In 1850, Annapolis (the capital) had scarcely three thousand inhabitants, including slaves, and the populations of the two cities in the west, Frederick and Cumberland, each barely exceeded six thousand. Under these circumstances, educational institutions tended to serve as cultural repositories. A notable example, the United States Naval Academy, founded in Annapolis in 1845, developed a lyceum in which it exhibited not only naval artifacts, but also works of art, including pictures by Chaplain George Jones.[22] In Emmitsburg (north of Frederick), Mount Saint Mary's College had formed by 1830 a "College Cabinet" which housed such curiosities as Daniel Webster's hat and a footprint of a dinosaur, as well as a number of pictures—including a *Triumphal Entry of Alexander into Babylon* from the studio of Charles Le Brun, given by John DuBois, who founded the college.[23]

Old Master paintings and works by Americans had dominated collections both locally and nationally during the first half of the nineteenth century. In the 1850s, however, a taste for contemporary European pictures began to emerge, presaging the trends in collecting that were to dominate the post-Civil War era. Contributing to this development was New York's ascendancy in the art market and the opening in that city of a number of establishments specializing in contemporary European art—among them the Dusseldorf Gallery, the International Art Union operated by Goupil, Vibert & Cie. of Paris, and offshoots of the Art Union, the galleries of William Schaus and W. Knoedler. Also active in promoting foreign art was the Belgian dealer, Ernest Gambart, who in 1857 circulated in America an exhibition of modern British paintings.[24] John Ruskin's critical writings, *Academy Notes* (1857–59) and *Modern Painters* (1846–60), were also popular at this time.

In Baltimore, William T. Walters was one of the earliest collectors to anticipate the shift in taste. At the outset of his career he had bought a Napoleonic subject by a minor Swiss painter, E. A. Odier, which he lent to the 1857 exhibition of The Maryland Historical Society, along with several more prosaic works, including copies after Salvator Rosa and Murillo. In addition, at this time, he promoted the careers of a number of local artists, among them William Henry Rinehart, the sculptor, and Alfred Jacob Miller, remembered for his oils and watercolors recording a trip to the American West in 1837. In the 1850s, Walters commissioned pictures from artists of national distinction, among them Asher B. Durand (then president of the National Academy of Design), Charles Loring Elliott, and John Kensett. At the second exhibition of paintings by English and French artists held at the National Academy of Design (in October 1859), however, Walters departed radically from his earlier interests and acquired J.-L. Gérôme's masterpiece, *The Duel After the Masquerade* (no.94), along with several paintings by P.-E. Frère and other protegés of Ernest Gambart and John Ruskin. That November, he also commissioned from the French figurative painter, Hugues Merle, *The Scarlet Letter,* a painting recording an incident from Nathaniel Hawthorne's novel of the same title. Acting as agent for the commission was a fellow Baltimorean, George A. Lucas, a resident of Paris for fifty-two years who was to play a significant role in facilitating the formation of a number of American collections of European art, especially in Baltimore.[25]

Cultural life revived more slowly in Maryland following the disruption of the Civil War than it did in the northern states. When the trustees of The Peabody Institute rode together in J. W. Garrett's private railroad car to Havre de Grace to greet George Peabody, who had come to attend the opening of his Baltimore institute in October 1866, it was the first such bipartisan gathering held since the end of hostilities.[26] Peabody, given the dearth of public institutions in Baltimore, intended the Institute to serve as an art gallery, in addition to providing a library, conservatory, and lecture hall. Not until 1873, however, when John W. McCoy donated the statue, *Clytie,* W. H. Rinehart's chef d'oeuvre, did The Peabody Institute begin to assemble a collection, and only in 1879, the year when exhibitions began to be held, did the Institute supplant the Historical Society as the city's principal art gallery.[27]

Meanwhile, in 1870, a committee of artists and amateurs determined to revive a Maryland Academy of Art, which would promote the appreciation of the fine arts with a program of "exhibitions, discourses and lectures." Quarters were located on Mulberry and Cathedral Streets, and a former dentist, A. J. Volck, who is remembered for his pro-Confederacy cartoons, was appointed director and sole instructor. No more successful than its predecessor, the Academy was dissolved within three years and its collection of plaster casts was transferred to the Peabody Gallery.[28]

Indicative of a growing interest in art in the 1870s was a series of exhibitions held to raise funds for two local charities, the Association for the Improvement of the Condition of the Poor and the Ladies' Relief Association. The first exhibition, lasting twelve days in the Fifth Regiment Armory in January 1874, proved to be a particularly gala event.[29] E. G. Lind, architect of The Peabody Institute, and a decorations committee were responsible for the array of evergreens, flowers, and cages of canaries that adorned the Armory. Music, including such selections as the *Napoleon March* and *Bauer und Dichter,* was provided by the bands of Fort McHenry and the Fifth Regiment. Many of the city's leading collectors were involved: an entire section was allotted to Colonel J. Stricker Jenkins' exhibition of European and American paintings; W. S. G. Baker lent a number of works, including A. J. Miller's *Lost Hunter;* and T. Harrison Garrett showed a *Coast Scene* by A. T. Bricher. Baltimore's major dealers participated, with the firm of Bryer and Bendann contributing a display of sculpture groups by John Rogers, and Myers and Hedian showing their stock of Dresden and Sèvres porcelain. This and subsequent Charity Art Exhibitions proved to be financial successes but were not uniformly well received. John R. Tait, writing for *Lippincott's Magazine* in 1883, ranked Baltimore "at the bottom of the list of American towns" in art exhibitions. He observed that the shows benefited some local charity rather than "art" and caustically observed that "when such entertainments are supplemented by music, lunch-rooms, and flower-stands, and, above all, are made fashionable, it is possible to bring together some hundreds of people to look—at each other."[30] About 1876, William T. Walters assumed the task of raising funds for the Poor Association, opening his house and gallery to the public several days a week each spring. Proceeds from the fifty-cents admission went to the charity (fig. 2).

In Baltimore during the late nineteenth century, a surge of interest in the fine arts was manifested in the emergence of numerous art associations and institutions: the Decorative Art Society began to hold classes and exhibitions in 1878; the Sketch Club, begun in the winter of 1883/84, developed the following year into the Charcoal Club, a group of artists and laymen, headed initially by the collector John W. McCoy, who wished to paint and draw from live models; and, in 1899, a number of concerned Baltimoreans met at the residence of Theodore Marburg on Mount Vernon Place to found the Municipal Arts Society, an organization dedicated to beautifying the city, particularly through the placement of sculptural and pictorial decoration.[31]

Art collections, particularly in the field of contemporary European production, proliferated in the United States following the Civil War. The major collections, centered primarily in New York and Philadelphia and, to a lesser extent, in Boston, Cincinnati, St. Louis, and San Francisco, were described at length by Edward Strahan in his lavish, three-volume publication, *The Art Treasures of America.* In Baltimore, he observed,

> There are several parlor collections of great interest among the splendid homes of this ancient and beautiful city, where the warm enthusiasm of the South finds itself hospitable to every form and development of art, in distinction from the dilettante clannishness of the North—too prone to make fetishes of its Millets and Corots.[32]

Among the parlor collections that he noted was that of John W. Garrett, president of the B&O Railroad. Strahan cited twenty-three paintings in the Garrett collection—including several by the Americans F. E. Church, John Kensett, and Thomas Cole—and the remainder by then-fashionable European painters such as Gustave Brion, A. Schelfhout, and Georges Clairin. Other collectors Strahan regarded as worthy of mention were David T. Buzby and George Small, both commission merchants, George B. Coale and James Carey Coale, insurance company executives, and Dr. George Reuling, Charles J. Bonaparte, and John W. McCoy. Had they not recently been dispersed, Strahan unquestionably would have discussed the holdings of European and American paintings gathered by the late Colonel J. Stricker Jenkins, which were once rated as the city's second major collection.[33] As it was, he displayed unusual candor in denigrating the alleged masterpiece of the collection, Bouguereau's *Art and Literature* (no.33):

> The smoothness and finish . . . are equal to that of the most highly polished sculpture, and whoever loves exalted refinement
> for its own sake, divested of imagination and originality, will have a feast in this effort of Bouguereau at allegory.[34]

Only one collection, that of William T. Walters, did Strahan regard as warranting individual attention. While abroad during the Civil War, Walters sold many of his previous holdings and turned to the Paris art market, relying on George A. Lucas as a liaison with artists and dealers. On his return to Baltimore, Walters continued to augment the collection with European landscapes and academic genre subjects, works distinguished less by costliness than by selectivity. Masterpieces such as Meissonier's *1814* (no.95) and Gérôme's *Duel After the Masquerade* (no.94) appear modest in scale and composition when compared to works by those same artists in the collections of the New York magnates, A. T. Stewart and W. H. Vanderbilt. Altogether, Walters acquired more than 162 paintings by Europeans. In addition, he compiled a number of portfolios of watercolors and drawings. Gavarni, Léon Bonvin, Honoré Daumier and J.-F. Millet were some of the most notable artists to whom the collector was particularly drawn.

Among his contemporaries in both Europe and America, however, Walters was most noted as the patron of the French animalier, Antoine-Louis Barye. As early as 1863, Walters frequented Barye's studio, buying from the artist various watercolors and bronzes. In the early 1870s, in his capacity as chairman of the acquisitions committee of the Corcoran

Figure 2. *The picture gallery of William T. Walters was located behind the family residence on Mount Vernon Place. This photograph was taken about 1884.*

Figure 3. *William T. Walters' oriental collection was displayed in a room connecting his residence to the picture gallery. The photograph was taken about 1884.*

Gallery, Washington, DC, Walters commissioned a cast of every available subject, a move that resulted in the sculptor's oft-cited remark, "My own country has not done this much for me." In conjunction with the opening of a "Barye Room" in his Mount Vernon Place residence in February 1885, Walters presented the City of Baltimore with Barbedienne reductions of the allegorical groups, *War, Peace, Order,* and *Force,* of the Louvre's *Cour de Carrousel,* as well as the duplicate of the *Seated Lion* of the Louvre's *Quai Gate.* Heading a committee of American admirers of Barye who wished to erect a monument to the sculptor on the Île Saint-Louis, Paris, Walters was primarily responsible for an exhibition held at the American Art Association in New York from November 1889 through January 1890, which afforded New Yorkers the opportunity of seeing not only a comprehensive selection of Barye's work in various media, but also one hundred paintings by the artist's friends. The show included works by the sculptor's early friends Géricault, Delacroix, and Corot (described as members of "the phalanx of 1830"), as well as some by his Barbizon associates.

Collections of various categories of art proliferated in Baltimore during the last three decades of the nineteenth

Figure 4. *This photograph of Doctor J. F. Goucher was taken about 1900. (Photograph courtesy of Goucher College.)*

Figure 5. *Among the works displayed in Dr. Crim's parlor at 413 West Fayette Street is a replica of Canova's statue of* The Three Graces *(at the left), which had belonged formerly to Major George Whistler, father of the artist, James Abbot McNeill Whistler.*

century. One of the more influential was William T. Walters' pioneer collection of Asian art. Enthralled by Sir Rutherford Alcock's display of oriental artifacts, shown at the International Exhibition in London in 1862, Walters turned to that field with the same zeal that characterized his pursuit of European painting. His forays in the market were abetted by visits to subsequent international exhibitions, particularly to the Viennese exhibition of 1873, at which he participated as a United States commissioner. By 1884, Walters had acquired more than fourteen hundred pieces of Chinese ceramics and twenty-three hundred Japanese works of art (fig. 3).[35]

Bibliophilic interests have flourished in Baltimore since the Library Company of Baltimore was founded in 1796. During the 1870s, collectors of books as works of art included John W. McCoy, reputed to have owned Baltimore's most extensive library, and Thomas Harrison Garrett, who initiated the now renowned holdings of Evergreen House with his library of rare books, deluxe art folios, and Cruickshank illustrations. Not content with compiling a library of fine art books, William T. Walters undertook several noble publications: *Notes Critical and Biographical: Collection of W. T. Walters,* issued in 1895 by J. M. Bowles from the press of Carlon and Hollenbeck, Indianapolis, was one of the first ventures in typography and ornamental work by the American book designer, Bruce Rogers, while the catalogue of the oriental collection, *Oriental Ceramic Art,* which was published in 1897 with Louis Prang's 116 color lithographs—some the result of as many as thirty-two stones—has remained a landmark in American printing.[36] Much of this enthusiasm for fine books can be credited to John W. M. Lee, who served as librarian of the Mercantile Library Association from 1870 to 1885 and as librarian and as "Curator of the Cabinet" of The Maryland Historical Society from 1877 to 1892. Not only was Lee consulted by local bibliophiles, but he also served as an agent for a number of their acquisitions.[37]

With the openings of The Johns Hopkins University in 1876 and the Women's College (later Goucher College) in 1884, scholars with a range of interests were drawn to Baltimore. As early as 1880, a number of Greek vases were presented to the Hopkins Archaeological Museum by Professors Frothingham and Emerson.[38] In the early twentieth century, this museum's holdings were augmented with a number of gifts, purchases, and loans, including a unique collection of Graeco-Roman medical instruments unearthed at Colophon, Turkey. Among the major bequests were a number of Egyptian artifacts left by James Teackle Dennis, who had studied Egyptology from 1896 to 1903 and had participated in excavations of the burial complex of Mentuhotep, at Deir el-Bahari, from 1905 to 1907 (nos. 72–80). Following the opening of a museum at the Women's College in 1889, Dr. J. F. Goucher (fig. 4), the Methodist educator who had played an important role in the founding of the institution, presented a selection of antiquities from his personal collection, including Egyptian objects purchased through Emil Brugsch, assistant curator of the Cairo Museum, and some pre-Columbian sculpture (nos. 36–42).[39]

Figure 6. *The Main Gallery of The Crescent Democratic Club, Baltimore, is shown as it was in 1905.*

Sanitary fairs featuring American antiques and relics were held during the Civil War to raise money for the sick and wounded. These exhibits, followed in 1875/76 by the Centennial celebrations, sparked an interest in the country's past and its early artifacts. Soon antiquarians specializing in wares of the Colonial and Revolutionary periods emerged, especially in New England. In Maryland, isolated instances of this fascination with the country's history can be identified. Robert Gilmor, Jr., for example, was proud to own as a "curious relic," Charles Willson Peale's painting, *Washington and the Generals at Yorktown,* as well as a tombstone from Jamestown.[40] Baltimore's preeminent collector of Americana at this time was the ebullient Dr. William Crim, a physician and surgeon of the Fifth Regiment Infantry. With an apparent disregard for aesthetic considerations, the doctor gathered a remarkable assemblage of material, including some fine paintings, sculpture, and early furniture, as well as an extraordinary amount of bric-a-brac. For ten days in the spring of 1903 the local press entertained its readers with accounts of the liquidation of the vast estate (fig. 5).

The development of Great Master collecting, W. G. Constable observed, was "largely due to social and economic changes in the United States during the eighties and the nineties."[41] He noted that there was then "a class of extremely wealthy men who formed an aristocracy based on money, whose preeminence was widely recognized, and whose power was indisputable."[42] From these ranks came such individuals as J. P. Morgan, H. C. Frick, the Vanderbilts, John Wanamaker, and Collis P. Huntington, who collected the Great Masters and allied decorative arts at an unrivaled pace. In Baltimore, their nearest counterpart was Mary Frick Jacobs. Combining the wealth of her first husband, Robert Garrett, and the intellectual attainments of her second spouse, Dr. Henry Barton Jacobs, with her own astuteness and distinguished heritage, Mrs. Jacobs readily assumed her role as an arbiter of society in both Baltimore and in Newport, Rhode Island. To fulfill this role, she twice expanded her residence on Mount Vernon Place—Stanford White was the architect initially, and John Russell Pope supervised the second renovation. To provide the setting for her receptions, Mrs. Jacobs procured quantities of eighteenth-century-style furniture, porcelains, and table services. At least one room was designated as a picture gallery, and an impressive array of paintings was acquired—primarily through Blakeslee Galleries of New York and the firm of Eugene Fischof in Paris. More than mere household furnishings, the collection excelled in eighteenth-century French pictures and contained a number of important Old Master works.

A preponderance of Maryland collectors, individuals such as John W. McCoy, C. J. M. Eaton, and Robert Hall, were more modest in their aspirations and tended to confine themselves to paintings by contemporary American and (to a much lesser extent) European artists. Patronage of local talent was also, clearly, an objective for some, including Theodore Marburg, Faris C. Pitt, Dr. George Reuling, and James Wilkinson.[43]

Also notable were two quasi-institutional art collections accessible to the public at the turn of the century. James L. Kernan maintained a picture gallery in a corridor connecting the Kernan Hotel (later the Congress Hotel) with his theater, in which he displayed such paintings as Thomas M. Hemy's ten-by-twelve-foot work, *Every Soul Was Saved,* a Rembrandt Peale portrait of George Washington, and A. Robaudi's *After the Ball,* along with innumerable prints.[44] More ambitious was the Art Gallery of The Crescent Democratic Club on North Paca Street.[45] In a properly skylighted apartment, the Club showed more than 390 works in various media (fig.6), all contributed by the members who subscribed to the belief:

> Wherever there is a picture gallery there is a center from which flow to homes and families both culture and refinement, and the inmates learn to love adornment and to displace ugliness with beauty.[46]

The pictures in this unique institution were predominantly by contemporary American and British artists, though there were also several attributed to Francesco Albani and Gaspar Poussin.

Outside Baltimore there was still scant evidence of a serious commitment to art collecting. A notable exception, however, was Thomas C. Footer of Cumberland, who acquired a number of European paintings and porcelains. An admirer of William and Henry Walters, Footer emulated them by erecting a gallery at the rear of his residence, to house his art collection and library. According to family tradition, Footer's offer to donate the gallery and its contents to Cumberland was rejected because of the town's reluctance to assume responsibility for their maintenance.

The first thirty-four years of the twentieth century saw the establishment of permanent teaching facilities for the fine arts in Baltimore at the Mount Royal Avenue Branch of The Maryland Institute,[47] as well as the founding of the city's two principal art museums, The Walters Art Gallery and The Baltimore Museum of Art.

Henry Walters began to expand the range of his father's holdings as early as 1893 with some ancient Near Eastern cylinder seals purchased at the Chicago World's Fair (fig.7). His acquisition in 1902 of the contents of the Palazzo Accoramboni in Rome, however, dramatically transformed the scope of his collecting. Thereafter, Walters was committed to forming a collection that would illustrate artistic creativity through the ages—an objective which, in its breadth, distinguished him from contemporary collectors. The gallery that Walters bequeathed to Baltimore in 1931 was remarkable not only in its comprehensiveness, but also in the number of fields in which it excelled: Egyptian bronzes, Roman sculpture, Migration-period jewelry, medieval manuscripts, Renaissance paintings and decorative arts, eighteenth-century Sèvres porcelains, and nineteenth-century paintings, to cite but a few.

Meanwhile a number of citizens, including Henry Walters, who were concerned that Baltimore lagged behind other East Coast cities in establishing a municipal art museum, banded together to improve the situation. The Baltimore Museum of Art was incorporated in 1914, but not until eight years later did it find temporary housing in the former residence of Mary Garrett, at the southwest corner of Mount Vernon Place and Cathedral Street.[48] A director was appointed and a permanent collection was begun with Dr. A. R. L. Dohme's gift of a painting of a coy, nude child on a sofa, by the English painter, W. S. Kendall. In February 1923, a series of loan exhibitions was initiated, with works borrowed from local collectors. Six years later, the museum moved to its Wyman Park site.

Figure 7. *This posthumous portrait of Henry Walters was painted in 1938 by Thomas C. Corner (1865–1938).*

Figure 8. *Jacob Epstein is shown on a visit to Hong Kong in 1925. (Photograph from Lester S. Levy,* Jacob Epstein *⟨Baltimore, 1978⟩.)*

Today, the institution serves as a monument to the achievements of Baltimore's collectors during the early twentieth century. Outstanding among them was Jacob Epstein (fig. 8), an immigrant from Lithuania who parlayed a dry-goods business into a giant department store, and, with the resulting fortune, assembled a remarkable array of Old Master paintings. Under the aegis of Sir Joseph Duveen and Knoedler and Co., the preeminent New York art dealers at that time, Epstein acquired such works as Van Dyck's *Rinaldo and Armida* and Justus Susterman's *Portrait of a Nobleman of the Medici Court,* as well as a number of bronzes by the nineteenth-century sculptors A. Rodin and A.-L. Barye. He lent his collection to The Baltimore Museum of Art in 1929, to mark the opening of its new building; later, Epstein bequeathed his collection to the museum.

The Epstein pictures, together with Mary Frick Jacobs' collection (given in 1938), as well as a number of eighteenth-century portraits left in 1944 by Elise Agnus Daingerfield, constitute the basis of The Baltimore Museum of Art's holdings of historical European painting. The nineteenth-century section was dramatically enriched by the gift of the Eisenberg Collection. Though it was not presented until 1967, the collection can be traced to about 1914. Abram Eisenberg, a native of Hungary, was raised in Lonaconing, Western Maryland. Coming to Baltimore, Eisenberg befriended Jacob Epstein, established his own retail house, Eisenberg's Underselling Store, and began to collect paintings. Initially directing his attention to the fashionable Barbizon and Hague schools, Eisenberg subsequently turned boldly to the Impressionists, acquiring two major Monets and a Renoir. Other fields were developed through further donations: among them, the Garrett family's gift of its print collection in 1930 and, three years later, Mrs. Miles White, Jr.'s gift of her silver.

Through the generosity of Claribel and Etta Cone and of Saidie A. May, The Baltimore Museum grew to excel in twentieth-century European art. The Cone sisters became acquainted with Matisse and Picasso as early as 1905/06, and, with the encouragement of members of the Stein family, they began to collect the works of these masters. The Cones' roles as independent collectors of the highest order, however, was assured in 1926 by Claribel's purchase at the John Quinn Sale of Matisse's controversial masterpiece, *The Blue Nude.* Described as works of "the extreme modernists" by one critic,[49] and as "far too good for Baltimore" by an official of another museum,[50] the Cone collection, when bequeathed to the museum in 1949, catapulted Baltimore into the twentieth century.

Mrs. May, with extraordinary altruism, committed herself to acquiring works of art from every historical period, a practice that she deemed appropriate in serving the requirements of the museum as a teaching institution, particularly with regard to children's exhibitions. These works she donated in 1933. Afterwards, she turned to contemporary art, buying pictures by artists associated with Cubism and Surrealism, fields that were ignored by the Cones.

   The Taste of Maryland closes with the year 1934, the date of the opening of The Walters Art Gallery as a public institution. The country was then in the midst of the Great Depression, and a chapter in the history of American art collecting had come to a close. By then, however, the course of development of our cultural institutions had been assured.

William R. Johnston
Associate Director/
Curator of 18th- and 19th-Century Art
The Walters Art Gallery

---

1. J. Thomas Scharf, *History of Baltimore City and County* (Philadelphia, 1881), 674. Hereafter cited as "Scharf, 1881."

2. William Eddis, *Letters from America* (London, 1792), 20, 112–13.

3. *Two Hundred and Fifty Years of Painting in Maryland*, exh. cat., The Baltimore Museum of Art, 11 May–17 June 1945.

4. Lillian B. Miller, *Patrons and Patriotism, The Encouragement of the Fine Arts in the United States, 1790–1860* (Chicago, 1966), 12–14.

5. William Dunlap, *A History of the Rise and Progress of the Arts of Design in the United States* (Boston, 1918), 3:27.

6. Eugenia Calvert Holland, "Riversdale, the Stier-Calvert Home," *Maryland Historical Magazine* 45(1950):271–94.

7. Letter from Stier to his daughter, Rosalie Eugenie, cited by Holland, "Riversdale," p.23, n.7.

8. Dunlap, *Arts of Design.* The writer is indebted to Susan G. Pearl, Research Historian, History Division, The Maryland–National Capital Park and Planning Commission, for sharing her findings regarding the Stier collection.

9. Miller, *Patrons and Patriotism*, 130.

10. "Unpublished Letters," *Maryland Historical Magazine* 26(1931):132.

11. In Philadelphia, "The Columbianum," an artists' organization, was founded in 1794, the Pennsylvania Academy in 1805, and the Athenaeum in 1814. Among the early institutions in New York were The Society of Fine Arts (later the American Academy of Fine Arts), started in 1802, The New-York Historical Society (1804), and the National Academy of Design (1825). The Massachusetts Historical Society opened in Boston in 1791 and the Boston Athenaeum in 1807.

12. Peale's museum is discussed at length by Wilbur H. Hunter, Jr., in *Rendezvous for Taste, Peale's Baltimore Museum, 1814–1830,* (Baltimore, 1956).

13. Joseph W. Cox, "The Origins of the Maryland Historical Society: A Case Study in Cultural Philosophy," *Maryland Historical Magazine* 74(1979):112.

14. *The Baltimore Sun* (8 September 1838), 2.

15. Scharf, 1881, 674.

16. J. Thomas Scharf, *The Chronicles of Baltimore* (Baltimore, 1874), 510–11, 525–26. Hereafter cited as "Scharf, 1874."

17. Catalogues were published in 1848, 1849, 1850, 1853, 1854, 1856, 1857, 1861, 1875, 1876, 1879, 1883, 1893, 1896, 1901, 1904, 1907, and 1908.

18. Robert Gilmor, Jr., as a collector is discussed by Anna Wells Rutledge in "Robert Gilmor, Jr., Baltimore Collector," *Journal of The Walters Art Gallery* 12, (1949):19–39.

19. *Letters of Horatio Greenough to his brother Henry Greenough* (Boston, 1887), 36.

20. *Catalogue of a very Celebrated and Valuable Collection of Gold, Silver and Copper Coins and Medals, The Property of Colonel M. I. Cohen of Baltimore*, exh. cat., Messrs. Bangs, Merwin & Co. (New York, 1875).

21. The plants are cited by Edith Rossiter Bevan in "Gardens and Gardening in Early Maryland," *Maryland Historical Magazine* 45(1950):259, and the violins are mentioned in "A Century of Baltimore Collecting, 1840–1940," The Baltimore Museum of Art (Baltimore, 1941), 13.

22. Information was provided by James W. Cheevers, Curator, United States Naval Academy Museum.

23. Information was provided by Professor Kelly Fitzpatrick, Director, Special Collections House, Mount Saint Mary's College.

24. Jeremy Maas, *Gambart, Prince of the Victorian Art World* (London, 1975), 95–97.

25. Lucas and Walters are discussed in *The Diary of George A. Lucas, An American Agent in Paris, 1857–1909*, transcribed and with introduction by Lilian M. C. Randall (Princeton, 1979), and William R. Johnston, *The Nineteenth Century Paintings in the Walters Art Gallery* (Baltimore, 1982).

26. Franklin Parker, *George Peabody, A Biography* (Nashville, 1971), 57–58. The Peabody Institute was incorporated in 1857 but not opened until 1866.

27. Anna Wells Rutledge, *List of Works of Art in the Collection of The Peabody Institute* (Baltimore, 1949).

28. Scharf, 1881, 674–75.

29. *The Baltimore Sun* (20 January 1974), 4; (21 January), 18.

30. John R. Tait, "Art in Baltimore," *Lippincott's Magazine* (November 1883):531–32.

31. The Decorative Art Society and the Charcoal Club are discussed in J. H. Hollander, *Guide to the City of Baltimore* (Baltimore, 1893), 101–03. Warren Wilmer Brown, in *The Municipal Art Society* (Baltimore, n.d.), outlines the goals of the Society. Meredith Janvier, in *Baltimore in the Eighties and Nineties* (Baltimore, 1933), recalls the Charcoal Club and its members who, in the halcyon era of the nineties, included many of the city's principal artists and collectors (pp.118–35).

32. Edward Strahan (Earl Shinn), *The Art Treasures of America* (Philadelphia, n.d. ⟨c.1879–80⟩), 3 vols., 3:75.

33. George Howard, *The Monumental City, Its Past History and Present Resources* (Baltimore, 1873), 71–72.

34. Strahan, *Art Treasures of America*, 76–77.

35. *Oriental Art of W. T. Walters* (Baltimore, 1884), xii.

36. Dorothy Miner, "The Publishing Ventures of a Victorian Connoisseur," *The Papers of the Bibliographical Society of America* 77, 3(1963):271–311.

37. Ruth Lee Briscoe, "John W. M. Lee," *Maryland Historical Magazine* 32, 1(1937):1–9.

38. David M. Robinson, "The Archaeological Museum at The Johns Hopkins University," *Art and Archaeology* 19, 5–6(1925):265–67.

39. Elizabeth Stillinger, *The Antiquers* (New York, 1980), 4–16.

40. Rutledge, "Robert Gilmor, Jr.," 28.

41. W. G. Constable, *Art Collecting in the United States of America* (London, 1964), 97.

42. Ibid.

43. Janvier, *Baltimore in the Eighties and Nineties,* 126.

44. Tom White, "Only the Painting Was Saved," *The News-American* (Baltimore, 29 April 1983), 6A.

45. Walter E. McCann, *The Art Club of the Crescent Democratic Club* (Baltimore, 1905), and *The Baltimore Sun* (24 June 1915), 12 (announcing the sale of the collection).

46. McCann, 10.

47. The Maryland Institute had been founded in 1826 as a school for the mechanical arts comparable to Philadelphia's Franklin Institute. Following the Baltimore Fire in 1904, the institution's responsibilities were divided—the mechanical arts were relegated to a building in Market Place, and the fine and practical arts to Mount Royal Avenue.

48. The early history of The Baltimore Museum of Art is discussed by Kent Roberts Greenfield in "The Museum: Its Half Century," *Annual I* (The Baltimore Museum of Art, 1966).

49. Thomas C. Corner, "Private Art Collections of Baltimore," *Art and Archaeology* 19, 5–6(1925):244.

50. Alfred Barr, director of The Museum of Modern Art, New York, quoted by Kent Roberts Greenfield, *Annual I*, 58.

ROBERT GILMOR, JR.   (1774–1848)
Baltimore

Successful trading ventures with the American colonies in 1767 and 1769 persuaded Robert Gilmor, Sr. (1748–1822), to emigrate from his native Scotland. After settling in Baltimore, he became eminent in the world of international commerce, initiating American trade with India and sending the first American merchant ship to Russia in 1784. He eventually established the great "Compting House" of Robert Gilmor & Sons, with a fortune estimated to amount, at its peak, to more than a million dollars.

Through the international milieu of his youth, Robert Gilmor, Jr., acquired cosmopolitan values, and his wealth enabled him to become the prototypical American merchant-prince. In his obituary he was praised as "a virtuous and public minded citizen—a liberal and enlightened Merchant—a munificent patron of the arts, with the tastes and acquirements of an accomplished gentleman . . . " (*Baltimore American,* 2 December 1848).

Educated in Amsterdam and Marseilles, as well as in Baltimore, and widely traveled, the younger Gilmor shared the interests prevalent among the educated people of his time. In addition to patronizing several societies for the advancement of the arts and sciences, he was an inveterate collector whose interests encompassed pictures, a library, minerals, autographs, engravings, drawings, and various works of art. Severe financial setbacks in the years preceding his death prevented him from fulfilling his wish of leaving his collections to a public institution in order to "diffuse a taste for works of art . . . "

An amateur draftsman himself, at the age of twenty-five, Gilmor already felt "a strong attachment to the Arts." He remarked, "My fondness for the subject may prove dangerous, but as long as I can restrain it with[in] the bounds of prudence and reason, I am convinced it will prove one of the greatest sources of pleasure, amusement and relaxation from the serious concerns of life." (Gilmor MS, "Memorandums made in a Tour of the Eastern States in the Year 1797"). Although he exercised discretion, his zest for collecting made Gilmor the most important American collector of his time.

His diverse collection, the first of its kind in America, included illuminated manuscripts, Classical artifacts, Old Master and contemporary paintings, drawings, and engravings, and European and American autographs. As a patron, he encouraged the rise of the Hudson River School of landscape painting, purchasing many works by Doughty, including *A View of Baltimore from Beech Hill* (no.10), his country estate, and plying Thomas Cole with financial assistance and professional advice. Early on, Gilmor recognized the talent of the Neoclassical sculptor, Horatio Greenough. Gilmor commissioned a portrait bust of his wife from the young Bostonian, helped raise a subscription to send the artist to Italy, and commissioned *Medora* (no.11), Greenough's first monumental work.

Gilmor acquired paintings directly from artists and from dealers in America and Europe. Familiar with contemporary authorities such as Gilpin, Burke, and Winckelmann, and an enthusiastic visitor of private and public collections, Gilmor—like all amateurs of the period—prided himself on his taste. Writing from Amsterdam in 1800, he remarked, "I am become so great a connoisseur, that I can instantly on entering a room point out even from the door all the principal pictures." ("Journal of Travels," 4 August 1800). As his attribution to Holbein of a painting now ascribed to Corneille de Lyon (no.2) testifies, Gilmor's connoisseurship was limited by contemporary knowledge. Similarly, the collecting habits of his European counterparts are echoed in the prevalence of Flemish and Italian paintings in Gilmor's collection. Beyond the sheer mass of objects he acquired, however (an inventory lists 225 paintings and 25 portfolios of drawings and engravings alone), Gilmor's habit of maintaining systematic records marks him as an exceptional collector: " . . . I make a point of preserving in a packet by themselves, receipts for purchases of pictures stating what the picture is or is supposed to be, and who painted it, with as full a history of it as is known to the seller . . . It gives an authenticity and interest to your collection when you can trace a picture back as far as possible . . . " (letter to Charles Graff, 20 September 1830, Metropolitan Museum of Art, New York).

Gilmor's catalogue raisonné is now lost, and currently available information makes it almost impossible to trace the subsequent history of much of his collection. The works that can be identified as belonging to Gilmor, however, make it possible to accept his own assessment of his accomplishment. Surveying the objects acquired during a lifetime of collecting, he observed: "It is no doubt equal if not superior to most in the country, yet one good picture of a London cabinet would be worth the whole—I have however seen much worse collections abroad, and if mine only stimulates my countrymen to cultivate a taste for the Fine Arts I shall be well compensated for my expense in making it even such as it is" (letter to Graff).

Suggestions for Further Reading: Robert Gilmor, Jr., "Memorandums made in a Tour of the Eastern States in the Year 1797," reprinted in *Bulletin of the Boston Public Library* 11, 1 (April 1892):75–76; William Dunlap, *A History of the Rise and Progress of the Arts of Design in the United States* (Boston, 1918), 3:272–75; Barbara Novak, "Thomas Cole and Robert Gilmor," *Art Quarterly* 25, (1962):41–53; Nathalia Wright, "Horatio Greenough, Boston Sculptor, and Robert Gilmor, Jr., His Baltimore Patron," *Maryland Historical Magazine* 51, (1956):1–13; *Letters of Horatio Greenough to His Brother Henry Greenough*, ed. F. B. Greenough (Boston, 1887); Anna Wells Rutledge, "Robert Gilmor, Jr., Baltimore Collector," *Journal of The Walters Art Gallery* 12 (1949):19–39; W. R. Rearick, "Some Little Known Old Master Drawings in the Baltimore Museum of Art,"—Studies in Honor of Gertrude Rosenthal, part 2, *Baltimore Museum of Art Annual* 4 (1972); Francis C. Haber, "Robert Gilmor, Jr.—Pioneer American Autograph Collector," *Manuscripts* 7, 1 (Fall 1954):13–17.

———*B.B.*

1 BOOK OF HOURS
French, c.1420
Tempera and gold on parchment
5 ¼ x 4 inches
Lent by the Library of Congress (MS 92)

The taste for illuminated manuscripts among American collectors finds important expression in this prayerbook, which was inscribed by its purchaser in 1807, "Robert Gilmor Jun'r." A Paris usage is indicated by the contents of the calendar, the Office of the Virgin (incomplete), and the Office of the Dead, which opens with a rubric actually specifying its *lusaige de Paris*. Five extant miniatures further attest to this origin, reflecting in style, compositional devices, and palette the marked influence of the noted Parisian workshop headed by the Boucicaut Master. Specific motifs linking the Gilmor Hours with earlier productions from this atelier include diminutive angels in the background of several of the miniatures. Shown in pairs, one set holds a curtain serving as a backdrop for the Annunciation to the Virgin, while in the Nativity scene an angelic duo underscores the sacred import of Christ's birth.

The illuminator's awareness of mainstream developments is further reflected in details such as the book-satchel carried by the Virgin's handmaiden in the Visitation scene, an adaptation of the depiction of the book held by the Virgin in the analogous miniature in John, duke of Berry's *Très Riches Heures*. The realistic depiction of a man's corpse below the judgment of his soul at the beginning of the Office of the Dead, on the other hand, not only harks back to the comparable miniature in the duke's *Belles Heures* but also anticipates the monumental treatment of the theme in the *Rohan Hours* and its descendants.

Provenance: Purchased by Robert Gilmor, Jr., in Charleston, South Carolina, 1807; J. M. Winkler, Baltimore; acquired by the Library of Congress, 1922

Selected References: De Ricci, *Census* 1:235, no.120; Millard Meiss, *French Painting in the Time of Jean de Berry: The Boucicaut Master* (London, 1968), 137, 147⁵⁷, figs.165, 296–98; Meiss, *French Painting in the Time of Jean de Berry: The Limbourgs and Their Contemporaries* (New York, 1974), 271, fig.879.

———————————————————————————*L.M.C.R.*

CORNEILLE DE LYON
Dutch-French, 1500/10–75

2 (?) *Portrait of Charles, duc de Cossé-Brissac* (1525–30)
Oil on panel
6 ⅜ x 5 ¼ inches
Lent by the Memorial Art Gallery, University of Rochester, Marion Stratton Gould Fund

In 1551, the Venetian ambassador, Giovanni Capelli, described a visit to Corneille's studio, where he saw portraits of the members of the French court (Etienne Moreau-Nélaton, *Les Clouet et leurs émules*, Paris, 1924, 1:92). The chronicler, Brantôme, also described a 1564 visit by Catherine de Médicis to "a painter by the name of Corneille, who'd in a large room all the great lords, princes, cavaliers, princesses, dames, and daughters of the Court of France." (*Oeuvres de Pierre de Bourdeille de Brantôme,* ed. L. Lalanne. Paris, 1874, 7:343–44). On the basis of these contemporary references, it has become traditional to assign to Corneille de Lyon a group of small, half-length panel portraits dating about 1530–70, showing members of the French nobility. Recent evidence suggests that he also painted wealthy members of the third estate. Attribution of specific paintings to the hand of the master is made difficult by the replicas emanating from his workshop, in which his son (also named Corneille) and a daughter participated.

The presumed subject of the portrait is Charles, duc de Cossé-Brissac (1506–63), a gallant gentleman known among women as *le beau Brissac*. A distinguished soldier, as well as a diplomat, he became *colonel général de l'infanterie française* in 1542, *grand maître de l'artillerie* in 1547, *maréchal de France* in 1550, and finally, *duc et gouverneur de Paris* in 1561. Charles de Cossé-Brissac is the subject of at least two other portraits by Corneille de Lyon: one in the Louvre (J. Guiffrey, *La Peinture au Musée du Louvre,* 1929, 1:47, fig.53); the other in the Metropolitan Museum of Art (C. Sterling, *Catalogue of French Paintings, XV–XVIII centuries,* 1955, 32–33). The count is also the subject of a miniature by Clouet in the Metropolitan Museum of Art, and of drawings in the Musée Condé, Chantilly.

1

2

3

CHRISTIAN VAN POL
Dutch, 1752–1813
3 *Lilacs*
Oil on canvas
10 ¾ x 8 ⅝ inches
Lent by the John G. Johnson Collection, Philadelphia

A student of the flower painter J. F. van Dael (1764–1840), van Pol was essentially a decorative artist. In 1782, he went to Paris to work as a designer at the Gobelins Manufactory. Four years later he began his most notable work—assisting van Dael in decorating the chateaux of Bellevue, Chantilly, and of Saint Cloud, where he specialized in decorative arabesques. Van Pol also decorated snuffboxes, miniatures, and porcelains.

Selected References: W. Valentiner, *Catalogue of a Collection of Paintings and some Art Objects* (Philadelphia, 1913), 2:182; *John G. Johnson Collection* (Philadelphia, 1972), 67.

——————————————— *B.B.*

Recently, Dr. Aldo Caporale has suggested that the sitter in the Rochester panel is Charles 1er de Cossé, comte de Brissac (1508–64) and that the portrait, by an anonymous artist, dates from about 1528.

Provenance: Adolph-Ulrich Wertmüller Sale, 18 May 1812 as "French Noblesse"; P. Flandin; 1821, Robert Gilmor, Jr. (attributed to Hans Holbein); acquired from a collateral descendant of Gilmor by Robert Lebel, Paris; acquired 1947, Memorial Art Gallery of The University of Rochester

Selected Exhibitions: Maryland Historical Society, 1848 (as Holbein), 1856; "Treasures from Rochester," Wildenstein, New York, 1977

Selected References: William Dunlap, *A History of the Rise and Progress of the Arts of Design in the United States* (Boston, 1918), 3:274; Anna Wells Rutledge, "Robert Gilmor, Jr., Baltimore Collector," *Journal of The Walters Art Gallery* 12(1949):18–39, fig.11; Michel Benisovich, "Sale of the Studio of Adolph Ulrich Wertmüller," *Art Quarterly* 16, 1(1953):20–29, fig.2.

——————————————— *B.B.*

4

5

6

GIOVANNI BATTISTA PIRANESI
Italian, 1720–78
4 *Sketch for His Own Tomb* (1778)
Pen on paper
9 5/16 x 10 13/16 inches
Lent by The Peabody Institute of the City of
Baltimore: The Charles J. M. Eaton Collection

Characterized by A. Hyatt Mayor as a "passionate anatomist of ruins," Piranesi's fascination for architecture reflects his early education by his father, a stonemason, and by his uncle, an engineer and architect. Piranesi subsequently learned etching in Rome, returned to his native Venice and worked briefly in Tiepolo's studio, and finally settled in Rome in 1745. He became one of the city's most notable inhabitants, influencing the character of Neoclassicism as well as the development of the Empire style through his polemical writings on architecture, his publishing, his prints, and other commercial ventures.

The inscription on this drawing translates, "Drawn by the Cavaliere Piranesi to give you an idea for his own tomb. 12 May 1778," suggesting that Piranesi was already thinking of death before embarking on his (final) expedition to Paestum, where he made preparatory drawings for his last set of etchings. Using drawings almost exclusively as notes for his etchings, he sketched rapidly, explaining: "Don't you see that if my

drawing was finished, my plate would be a copy . . . " An architect as well as an antiquarian, he pictures himself seated and casually contemplative before the framed bas-relief of a colonnaded vista.

Inscription: *Disegno fatto dal Cav. Piranesi Per dar[s]i 1 idea del suo Deposito/Di 12 Maggio 1778*; below the margin of the drawing in two different hands, on the left: *Da Roma 1843*; on the right: *Roma, 1843*

Provenance: Robert Gilmor, Jr.; Charles J. M. Eaton; The Peabody Institute

Selected Reference: A. Hyatt Mayor, "Two Piranesi Drawings in the Gilmor Collection," *Baltimore Museum of Art News 20, 1* (October 1956):1–2.

—————————————————— *B.B.*

JEAN HONORÉ FRAGONARD
French, 1732–1806
5 *Temple in a Garden* (c.1760)
Pen and brown ink, brown and gray washes, and watercolor over black chalk on antique laid paper
5 3/4 x 8 1/4 inches
Lent by The Peabody Institute of the City of
Baltimore: The Charles J. M. Eaton Collection

Trained in the ateliers of Chardin and Boucher, the versatile Fragonard emerged as one of the greatest painters as well as one of the most delightful and original draftsmen of the eighteenth century. He won the Prix de Rome in 1752 but postponed leav-

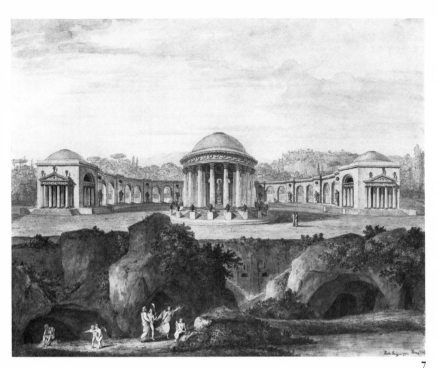

7

ing for Italy until 1755, and in the interim studied at the Ecole Royale des Elèves Protégés. At the Academy in Rome, he was encouraged by its director, Charles-Josèphe Natoire, who extended Fragonard's term as *pensionnaire* until 1761, providing him with the opportunity to refine his skill by working in conjunction with his fellow students, Greuze and Hubert Robert.

Landscape sketching *en plein air* was encouraged by Natoire. Stylistic evidence suggests that *Temple in a Garden* is an early experiment in the medium that Fragonard was later to master. Daubing wash over his rapidly executed chalk sketch, Fragonard emphasized the modulations of light and shade rather than the architectonic forms, creating a sense of atmosphere. Although probably invented, the scene combines a number of Roman motifs: the curved arcade in the background is reminiscent of the Tiburtine Fountain of the Villa d'Este, Tivoli, where Fragonard stayed during the summer of 1760.

Provenance: Robert Gilmor, Jr.; Charles J. M. Eaton; The Peabody Institute

Selected References: R. R. Bornemann, "The Gilmor Collection of Drawings—The French School," *The Baltimore Museum of Art News* 17, 5 (June 1954):10; Eunice Williams, *Drawings by Fragonard in North American Collections* (Washington, DC, 1978), 21–22, 34–35.

———————————————— *B.B.*

CIRCLE OF JOHN HAMILTON MORTIMER
British, 1740–79
6 *Old Man Haranguing Banditti* (c.1775–1800)
Pen and wash over pencil
11 ⁵⁄₁₆ x 9 inches
Lent by The Peabody Institute of the City of
    Baltimore: The Charles J. M. Eaton Collection

Mortimer, an inventive history painter and an influential and prolific graphic artist, studied with Thomas Hudson, Robert Edge Pine, and then with Cipriani at the duke of Richmond's sculpture gallery, where he won a prize for the best drawing after the antique, offered by the Society for the Encouragement of the Arts. Beginning in 1758, he studied at the Saint Martin's Lane Academy and, in 1764, won first prize for his history painting, *Saint Paul Preaching to the Britons* (Town Hall, High Wycombe). Although he was reputed to be "impudent in conduct and intemperate in his pleasures" (Edwards, 64), Mortimer served as vice-president and later as president of the Society of Artists, where he exhibited consistently from 1762 to 1777. He first exhibited at the Royal Academy in 1778 and was elected as an associate; unfortunately, he died before receiving his diploma.

Mortimer modeled his "bohemian" personality upon the romantic *persona* popularly ascribed to the Neapolitan artist, Salvator Rosa (1615–73). He was influenced

as well by Rosa's style and subject matter: "The favorite subjects of Mr. Mortimer's pencil were the representations of banditti, or those transactions recorded in history, wherein the exertions of soldiers are principally employed, as also incantations, the frolics of monsters, and all those kind of scenes that personify 'Horrible Imaginings'" (Edwards, 62–63). Although watercolors are less frequently encountered than pen-and-ink drawings in Mortimer's known oeuvre, *Old Man Haranguing Banditti* is characteristic of the pastiches after Rosa that Mortimer began to produce during the 1770s. In particular, Rosa's famous series of *Figurine* engravings for Carlo de'Rossi provided Mortimer with a convenient repertory of figures and poses. In the Gilmor watercolor, for example, the figure of the old man making hortatory gestures is derived directly from Bartsch XX.70, the seated figure in the foreground from Bartsch XX.37, and the armored figure behind the old man from Bartsch XX.49. The style of draftsmanship and wash technique suggest that an anonymous artist influenced by Mortimer is the author of this drawing.

Watermark: *IV*

Verso: Two sketches, in black chalk, of a seated male figure holding a staff and of a standing, robed figure; also an inscription in a later hand: *Drawn by Mortimer*

Provenance: Robert Gilmor, Jr.; Charles J. M. Eaton; The Peabody Institute

Selected References: A. Bartsch, *Le Peintre Graveur,* 21 vols. (Leipzig, 1870), 20:278ff.; Edward Edwards, *Andecdotes of Painters* . . . (London, 1808), 61ff.; John Sunderland, "John Hamilton Mortimer and Salvator Rosa," *Burlington Magazine* 112 (1970): 520–31; John Sunderland, "The Legend and Influence of Salvator Rosa in England in the Eighteenth Century," *Burlington Magazine* 115 (1973):785–89.

———————————————— *B.B.*

PIETRO BARGIGLI
Italian, second half of the 18th century–after 1814
7 *Allegory with Circular Temple* (1791)
Pen, brown ink, and watercolor on paper
17 ¹⁵⁄₁₆ x 22 ¾ inches
Lent by The Peabody Institute of the City of
    Baltimore: The Charles J. M. Eaton Collection

As his inscription indicates, Gilmor incorrectly attributed this drawing to Paolo Brizzio. Its actual author, Pietro Bargigli, is a little-known architect with Jacobin sympathies who held the title of Architetto del Consolato Romano in the short-lived Roman republic established by Napoleon. He was invited to Milan in 1801 to assist with

8

9

the decorations celebrating Napoleon's victories. Subsequently, the emperor's sister, Elisa Baciocchi, grand duchess of Tuscany, appointed him professor at the art academy of Carrara, where he taught architectural and ornamental drawing. He died a few years after his retirement in 1814.

In the foreground, Eros, holding a torch, and a winged Victory guide a young poet toward a path ascending to a circular temple of Apollo. Seated at the foot of the path, a genius holds the wreath of immortality. To the left, two putti mock the despairing, withered figure of Envy. A. Clark interprets the drawing as an "Allegory of the Poet Weaned from Envy or Uncontrolled Passion to True Imagination." The circular temple itself is reminiscent of the Round Temple at Tivoli; the cavernous foreground landscape recalls the Palatine Hill. Related to contemporary scenographic designs,

Bargigli's treatment of the scene is also typical of the Neoclassical architectural fantasies produced in the Roman milieu during the second half of the eighteenth century.

Inscription: (in the artist's hand, at lower left): *Pietro Bargigli fecit 1791;* (in Gilmor's hand, at lower right): *Paolo Brizzio 1791 Roma 18[43]* (?)

Provenance: Robert Gilmor, Jr.; Charles J. M. Eaton; The Peabody Institute

Selected References: A. Clark, "Roman Eighteenth Century Drawings in the Gilmor Collection," *Baltimore Museum of Art News* 24, 3(Spring 1961):5–12; Cleveland Museum of Art, *Neo-Classicism: Style and Motif,* exh. cat. (1964), no.164; Roberta Olson, *Italian Drawings 1780–1890,* exh. cat. (New York, 1980), no.20.

——————————————— *B.B.*

GILBERT STUART
American, 1755–1828
8 *George Washington* (1825)
Oil on canvas
30 ¼ x 25 ⅜ inches
The Walters Art Gallery (37.171)

Stuart produced three life portraits of George Washington (1732–99). His many copies of these portraits fall into three groups: the "Vaughan" type, after the 1795 portrait; the "Lansdowne" type, after the 1796 full-length portrait; and the "Athenaeum" type, produced during sittings in the autumn of 1797. Of these, the Athenaeum version proved the most popular. Stuart kept the original Athenaeum portrait and sold more than seventy copies, referring to them as his "hundred-dollar bills." Robert Gilmor commissioned this Athenaeum-type *George Washington* in 1825. It was the last replica Stuart produced, and Samuel P. Avery, referring to a lost note from the artist, wrote that Stuart had said, "painting it for such a distinguished amateur, he had taken especial pains with it . . ."

Provenance: Robert Gilmor, Jr.; Mr. and Mrs. Charles Gilmor, to 1869; H. N. Barlow (dealer), Washington, DC; purchased in 1872 by Mrs. Sarah Madelaine Vinton Dahlgren; acquired from Mrs. Dahlgren by William T. Walters through S. P. Avery, 1885

Selected References: Edward S. King and Marvin Ross, *Catalogue of American Works of Art* (Baltimore, 1956), no.34; Edward S. King, "Stuart's Last Portrait of George Washington: Its History and Technique," *Journal of The Walters Art Gallery* 9(1946):80–96.

——————————————— *B.B.*

JOHN WESLEY JARVIS
American, 1780–1840
9 *Self-Portrait*
Oil on canvas
18 x 13 ½ inches

The Walters Art Gallery, Gift of Baroness Giskra in memory of her father, John King, Jr., 1948 (37.2011)

Jarvis was brought from England to America at age five and was raised in Philadelphia. He trained with the engraver, Edward Savage, and moved to New York in 1802, where he pursued a successful and highly prolific career as a portraitist. Between 1810 and 1813, Jarvis worked in Baltimore, in partnership with Joseph Wood.

Remembered by a contemporary as having "large features, a dark turbid complexion . . . and a prodigious head" (Dickson, 216), this romantic self-portrait belies Washington Irving's description of Jarvis as "one of the queerist, ugliest . . . little creatures in the world" (Dickson, 127).

Provenance: William Gwynn, Baltimore; Robert Gilmor, Jr.; Robert Gilmor III, Baltimore; John King, Jr., 1875; Baroness Helen Giskra, Baltimore, 1897

Selected Exhibitions: Peale's Baltimore Museum, October 1–November 9, 1822, no.157; Apollo Association, New York, September, 1840, no.21; "Charity Exhibition," Baltimore Academy of Music, March 16–31, 1876, no.407.

Selected References: H. E. Dickson, *John Wesley Jarvis* (New York, 1949), 354, no.115; Anna Wells Rutledge, "Robert Gilmor, Jr., Baltimore Collector," *Journal of The Walters Art Gallery* 12(1949):26, no.50, fig.8.

——————————————— *B.B.*

THOMAS DOUGHTY
American, 1793–1856
10 *View of Baltimore from Beech Hill* (1822)
Oil on canvas
14 ¼ x 18 ¼ inches
Lent by the Museum of Fine Arts, Boston, M. and M. Karolik Collection

On a letter written by the artist to the collector on 18 November 1822, Robert Gilmor added the notation: "T. Doughty of Philadelphia a landscape painter of Talent. He painted several pictures for me among them two from my country seat Beech Hill." Gilmor grew disenchanted with Doughty's later landscapes, finding them mannered and lacking in realism.

This painting is one of two by Doughty showing Baltimore from this site. The other, in the Baltimore Museum of Art, is slightly smaller and varies in the disposition of the trees in the foreground.

Signed: *Doughty 1822*

Provenance: Robert Gilmor, Jr.; probably Robert Gilmor (nephew of the precedent), Sale: *Catalogue of the Very Valuable and Original Oil Paintings Being a Portion of the Collection of the Late Robert Gilmor,* Baltimore, 10 November 1863, lot 60, "View of Baltimore" ($25.00) or lot 61, "View of the Chesapeake Bay from Beech Hill" ($32.50) to J. H. Weitzner (New York, 1944).

HORATIO GREENOUGH
American, 1805–52

11 *Medora*
Marble
Height: 14 ½ inches; Length: 58 inches
Lent by The Cloisters Children's Museum, Baltimore

Encouraged by the painter, Washington Allston, to pursue his interest in sculpture, Greenough sailed for Italy in 1825, becoming the first American sculptor to study abroad. He worked briefly in Rome with the Danish Neoclassical master, Bertel Thorwaldsen, and subsequently worked in Florence with Lorenzo Bartolini; he lived in Florence until 1850.

Gilmor was satisfied with a bust that Greenough had made of his wife, and commissioned from the artist another statue. In 1831, Greenough informed his patron that he had "begun the study of a figure which I before mentioned to you the Medora as described by Byron in the corsair [*sic*]— Here I can unite beauty to touching interest . . . I can make it rich in drapery and can do what has not been done in Italy for many years—attempt to interest and charm the eye and mind with a female form without appealing to the baser passions . . . " (*Letters,* 78). The specific source of the image is Canto III, verse 20, of Lord Byron's *The Corsair:*

> In life itself she was so still and fair,
> That death with gentler aspect
>   withered there,
> And the cold flowers
>   her colder hand contained,
> In that last grasp as tenderly
>   were strained
> As if she scarcely felt,
>   but feigned a sleep,
> And made it almost a mockery
>   yet to weep . . .

In a letter of 12 December 1831, however, Greenough explained to Gilmor that "the soul of my figure—or what I wish should be such" was best expressed in Petrarch's *Trionfi della Morte:*

> Not as a flame which by force is spent
> But which by itself consumes itself.
>   (1.160–61) (*Letters,* 98)

The statue was completed in June 1832. When it arrived in America in October, Greenough's first "poetical" work was displayed in Boston, where it was praised as an example of "refined taste," exhibiting "the highest excellence of soul and sentiment" (Crane, 57)—although the nudity of the idealized figure disturbed modest viewers. In Baltimore the following fall, the statue was again exhibited publicly before it finally entered Gilmor's home. The collector was obliged to store it in his basement for lack of space. In the winter of 1837, however, his wife attended a fancy-dress ball as "Medora."

Provenance: Robert Gilmor, Jr., Sale: 10 November 1863, *Catalogue of the Very Valuable and Original Oil Paintings, being a portion of the Collection of the Late Robert Gilmor also Marble Statuary, Engravings, and Rare Works being sold by Public Auction, at the dwelling of Mr. William Gilmor:* "GREENOUGH—Celebrated figure of Medora—considered the finest piece of Sculpture in the Country" (p.5); Sumner Parker, Baltimore

Selected Exhibitions: Boston: October 1832; Baltimore: Fall 1833

Selected References: William Gerdts, *American Neoclassical Sculpture* (New York, 1973), 119, pl.132; Dunlap, *A History of the Rise and Progress of The Arts of Design in the United States* 3:275; Sylvia Crane, *White Silence* (Coral Gables, 1972), 55–58; Nathalia Wright, ed. *Letters of Horatio Greenough* (Madison, 1972), 60, 78, 84–85, 106, 119, 122, 127, 130, 133–36, 138, 145, 149, 159, 164–65, 190–91.

—————————————————— *B.B.*

WILLIAM JAMES HUBARD
Anglo-American, 1807–62

12 *Robert Gilmor, Jr.*
Oil on panel
20 x 14 ¾ inches
Lent by The Baltimore Museum of Art: Charlotte G.
    Paul Bequest Fund

Recalling a visit to Maryland in the summer of 1831, the English barrister, Godfrey T. Vigne, wrote:

> At Baltimore I visited the studios of two very promising young artists; Mr. Hubbard [*sic*], an Englishman, is certainly the better painter, but has the advantage of four or five years' experience over Mr. Miller who is an American, quite a boy, and whom I think at least an equal genius.
>   (*Six Months in
>   America,* 1, 141–42.)

Hubard, who had originally specialized in silhouette cutting, turned to oil painting after his arrival in this country. On three occasions he visited Baltimore—in the summer of 1825, again in 1830/32, and finally in

10

11

12

1837. The Gilmor portrait, thought to have been produced during the second visit, shows the collector surrounded by his possessions, including a Greek red-figure amphora and *kylix,* some scrolls, a portfolio of engravings and, scarcely discernible in the upper right, a marble bust on a wall bracket.

Provenance: Robert Gilmor, Jr.; by 1945 William L. Gilmor, Baltimore; Sam. W. Pattison & Co., Inc., Sale, Baltimore, 1956

Selected Exhibition: Third Annual Exhibition of the Washington Art Association, 1859, no.35

Selected References: Anna Wells Rutledge, "Robert Gilmor, Jr., Baltimore Collector," *Journal of The Walters Art Gallery* 12 (1949):18; Sona K. Johnston, *American Paintings 1750–1900 from the Collection of The Baltimore Museum of Art* (Baltimore, 1983), 84, no.64.

——————————— *W. R. J.*

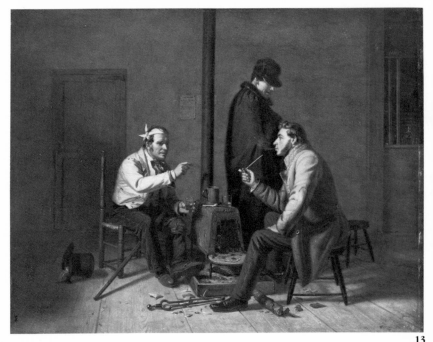

13

WILLIAM SIDNEY MOUNT
American, 1807–68
13 *The Long Story* (1837)
Oil on panel
17 x 22 inches
Lent by The Corcoran Gallery of Art, Washington, DC

The son of a Long Island tavern owner, Mount has portrayed a scene with which he was particularly familiar. In a letter to Robert Gilmor, Jr., he identified the figures in this "conversation piece" as the "tavern or store keeper" who among them was often a "General, or Judge or Postmaster"; an old invalid who was a "kind of Barroom Oracle"; and a traveler awaiting the arrival of a stage.

The Long Story exemplifies the wholesome, good-natured humor of the Long Island genre painter, whose comic scenes were widely popular.

Provenance: Purchased by Robert Gilmor, Jr., December 1837; acquired by William Corcoran before 1875

Selected Exhibitions: National Academy of Design, New York, 1838, no.308; Artists' Fund Society, Philadelphia, 1840, no.38

Selected References: W. Alfred Jones, "A Sketch of the Life and Character of William S. Mount," *American Whig Review* (August 1851):124; Charles J. Werner, "William S. Mount and his Art," *Historic Miscellanies Relating to Long Island* (Huntington, 1917), 34; Bartlett Cowdrey and Hermann Warner Williams, Jr., *William Sidney Mount, 1807–1868, An American Painter* (New York, 1944), 18, no.27.

——————————— *W. R. J.*

JOHNS HOPKINS   (1795–1873)
Baltimore

A name that stands out among the many lenders to The Maryland Historical Society's second annual exhibition, in 1849, is that of Johns Hopkins, the philanthropist who left funds for the establishment of the university and hospital in Baltimore that bear his name.

Leaving the family plantation, "Whitehall," on the Severn River in Anne Arundel County, Johns Hopkins moved to Baltimore to join the commission grocery business of an uncle, Gerard Hopkins. A disagreement with this relative involving commerce in whiskey, a violation of the family's Quaker principles, led Johns to establish his own firm, "Hopkins Brothers," a wholesale provisions house that conducted business in the valleys of Virginia and North Carolina. As he prospered, Hopkins diversified his interests, investing heavily in The Baltimore and Ohio Railroad. By 1847 he had become a director of the railroad, and in 1855 he was appointed chairman of its finance committee. Twice, in 1857 and again in 1873, Johns Hopkins pledged his personal fortune to save the line from bankruptcy.

Hopkins' contributions to the 1849 exhibition were modest. They included *The Sutler's Booth* (no.1), *Dido's Purchase* (no.135), and *Judith with the Head of Holofernes* (no.267), which were unattributed; as well as *Landscape* (no.235), given to F. Koken (perhaps Edmund Koken), and *Love and War,* a copy after Titian by the Baltimore painter, A. J. Miller. Also known to have belonged to Hopkins is a large view of Venice by Augustus Weidenbach, in The Maryland Historical Society.

Were it not for his early patronage of A. J. Miller, Johns Hopkins would be of only incidental interest in a survey of Maryland collecting. The portraits of Johns Hopkins and of his mother, Mrs. Samuel Hopkins, painted in 1832, were among Miller's few works commissioned prior to his European sojourn in 1833/34, and the *Love and War,* a copy of Titian's *Allegory of Alfonso d'Avalos* in the Louvre, is characteristic of the type of painting with which the artist hoped to earn a livelihood following his return to Baltimore. Unquestionably one of Miller's finest paintings is *The Trapper's Bride,* commissioned by Johns Hopkins in 1846 for $150.

Suggestion for Further Reading: Helen [Hopkins] Thom, *Johns Hopkins, A Silhouette* (Baltimore, 1929).

———*W.R.J.*

ALFRED JACOB MILLER
American, 1810–74

14   *The Trapper's Bride*   (1846)
Oil on canvas
35 ½ x 28 ½ inches
Lent by The Johns Hopkins Hospital, Baltimore

Using a "trail sketch" now in the Gilcrease Institute of American History and Art, Tulsa, Miller executed a number of paintings recalling this incident, which he witnessed on a journey to the Rocky Mountains in the summer of 1837.

Shown is the marriage of the "half-breed" François to an Indian girl. The trapper purchased his bride, paying her father $600—in guns ($100 each), horse blankets ($50 each), red flannel ($20 a yard), alcohol ($64 a gallon), and tobacco and beads.

Other versions of this subject are listed in *Alfred Jacob Miller: Artist on the Oregon Trail.*

Provenance: Purchased from the artist for $150 by Johns Hopkins, 15 February 1856; The Johns Hopkins Hospital

Selected References: *Alfred Jacob Miller: Artist on the Oregon Trail,* ed. Ron Tyler (Fort Worth, 1982), 271–72, no.191 E.

———————————————————*W.R.J.*

14

MENDES ISRAEL COHEN   (1796–1879)

Baltimore

Mendes Israel Cohen was born into what would become one of the most prominent Jewish families in Baltimore history. After her husband's death in 1803, Cohen's mother, Judith, moved with her seven children from Richmond to Baltimore, joining a small Jewish community—which by 1810 included only about fifteen families. The Cohens almost immediately distinguished themselves. Jacob established the banking firm of Jacob I. Cohen and Brothers, with offices on the northeast corner of Baltimore and Calvert Streets, and in 1826 was elected president of the Baltimore City Council. His brother David founded the Baltimore Stock Board, later to be known as the Baltimore Stock Exchange. In time, the family moved to Charles Street and owned a private burial ground on Saratoga Street.

In 1812, at the age of sixteen, Mendes served as a member of Nicholson's Fencibles, in defense of the Star Fort (Fort McHenry). During the bombardment, he provided assistance that was recognized in 1836, when he was belatedly appointed colonel. The war apparently interrupted his education permanently, because shortly thereafter, Mendes joined his brothers' banking operation, from which he retired in 1829. He then set forth on a six-year tour of Europe and the Levant, where he made the acquaintance of the viceroy of Egypt, Mehemet Ali, who facilitated Cohen's travels on the Nile in 1832. In his own *kangea*, Cohen embarked on a four-and-a-half-month voyage to the second cataract at Wady Halfa in Nubia. During the journey, Cohen and his Arab servant purchased cloth in a local bazaar and fashioned what was the first American flag ever seen upon the Nile. Copious letters home to his family recount colorful incidents of this trip, including an encounter at Luxor with French officers who were removing the obelisk that would become the celebrated focal point of the Place de la Concorde, Paris. Cohen also describes an appalling cholera epidemic that killed almost one-third of the population in Cairo alone.

Throughout his Egyptian journey, and particularly at Memphis and Thebes, Cohen acquired many antiquities, which were supplemented in 1835 by objects he purchased in London at the auction of Consul General Salt. Among Cohen's collection, which eventually totaled about seven hundred items, were bronze statuettes, amulets, rings, scarabs, and embalmed animals. This material represented the earliest private collection of Egyptian antiquities in the United States and was documented admirably in a meticulously annotated catalogue, in which Cohen recorded the provenance of each piece. The Cohen Collection acquired a further distinction in 1845, when it was used to illustrate a lecture delivered in Baltimore by George Robins Gliddon, former United States vice-consul to Cairo and the first individual to present lectures on Egyptology in the United States.

After his return to Baltimore in about 1835, Cohen participated in various civic and business affairs. He served as a member of the Maryland legislature from 1847 to 1848, and in this capacity presided over the meeting in which was established the Hebrew, now known as Sinai, Hospital. Cohen was also appointed a director of the Fireman's Insurance Company and of The Baltimore and Ohio Railroad Company. Throughout his lifetime, Cohen was an inveterate collector with wide-ranging interests; he amassed quantities of objects, most of which were dispersed at auction in New York in 1875. Cohen never married, and thus, at his death in 1879, the Egyptian collection passed on to his nephews Mendes Cohen and Dr. Henry M. Cohen, from whom the collection was acquired in 1884 by The Johns Hopkins University. Today, the material forms part of The Johns Hopkins University Archaeological Collection.

Descendants of Cohen's brothers and sisters were active in the Baltimore community well into the twentieth century and became closely linked by marriage to the Ettings, another prominent Jewish family in Baltimore. The last descendant of both families was Eleanor Cohen, who died in 1937.

Suggestions for Further Reading: Ellen Reeder Williams, *The Archaeological Collection of The Johns Hopkins University* (Baltimore, 1984); *The Sunday Sun* (Baltimore, 18 January 1976); *The Sun* (Baltimore, 4 January 1980). Cohen's letters to his family, his diary, and the catalogue of his collection are in The Maryland Historical Society. The American flag is owned by The Johns Hopkins University.

—*E. R. W.*

15

16

18

17

19

15 MODEL BOAT

Egyptian (Middle Kingdom), 2040–1786 B.C.

Painted wood

Length: 26 inches

Lent by The Johns Hopkins University, Archaeological
Collection (no. 3843)

Such boat models were characteristic gifts
found in Middle Kingdom tombs. This example, with high, pointed ends, has protec-
tive eyes painted on the bow. On the stern
end of the deck are four holes for posts to
hold a canopy. Three of the posts are preserved. Four figures were placed on the
boat. At the stern, behind the canopy, a male
is seated with knees drawn up. Facing the
structure is a squatting figure whose arms
are now missing. At the bow of the boat,
another figure stands facing the stern. His
left arm is extended forward; the right is
missing. Another standing figure belongs to
the crew, but its placement is no longer
certain. The bodies of the figures are
painted red; the kilts, white; the hair, black.
The hull of the boat is green, with a red-and-
white band along the gunwale. The lozenge
design painted on the gunwale over the eye
is typical.

—————————————————*J. V. C.*

16 HEAD REST

Egyptian (18th Dynasty), 1570–1349 B.C.

Fine-grained wood

Height: 7 ¼ inches

Lent by The Johns Hopkins University, Archaeological
Collection (no. 3945)

This particularly elegant example of the ancient Egyptian pillow is made in two pieces.
The curved top piece fits over a dowel on
the base. Since the base of the top is wider
than the upper portion of the base, one
section of the piece must be missing. Both
sections are decorated with broad vertical
flutes.

For a similarly fluted piece, see James F.
Romano, *Egypt's Golden Age: The Art of*

*Living in the New Kingdom, 1558–1085
B.C.,* Museum of Fine Arts (Boston, 1982),
74, 75, no. 46.

—————————————————*J. V. C.*

17 APPLIQUÉ

Egyptian

Yellowish wood, covered with gesso and painted

Height: 6 ½ inches; Thickness: 1 ⅛ inches

Lent by The Johns Hopkins University, Archaeological
Collection (no. 3949)

This is one of a set of four plaques of roughly
square shape, on which a head has been
carved. The delicate features of the deeply
dimpled face are finely carved and covered
with gesso, painted red. The elaborate decoration of the wig is depicted in red and
black paint. The design on the wig appears
to represent a winged scarab. There are two
dowels at the top of the head and two at the
bottom, to connect the piece to something—perhaps a coffin. The faces are usually carved separately from the wigs.

—————————————————*J. V. C.*

18 WRITING KIT

Egyptian

Wood (painted?)

Length: 13 ⅞ inches; Thickness: ½ inch

Lent by The Johns Hopkins University, Archaeological
Collection (no. 3912)

This example of a scribe's writing case is
very well preserved. At one end are two
circular depressions for red and black ink,
surrounded by an incised cartouche frame.
Nine reed pens are still in the tapered slot
designed to hold them. A groove along the
edge of the slot suggests that the case once
had a lid.

—————————————————*J. V. C.*

19 USHABTI

Egyptian

Painted wood

Height: 14 ⅜ inches

Lent by The Johns Hopkins University, Archaeological
Collection (no. 3841)

A mummified figure is placed on a wooden
base, one end of which has been roughly
hollowed out for the insertion of another
figure. A blue, net pattern is painted over
the red wrappings. The elaborate collar
necklace is depicted in black paint on a
yellow surface, and an inscription runs
down the back pillar.

—————————————————*J. V. C.*

ARTIST UNKNOWN
French (?), early 1830s
20 *Portrait of Mendes Israel Cohen*
Oil on paperboard
12 ⁷⁄₁₆ x 9 ¾ inches
Lent by The Maryland Historical Society, Bequest of
Mrs. Harriet Cohen Coale

This portrait shows Cohen in the Turkish garb that he adopted during his travels in the eastern Mediterranean during the early 1830s.

Provenance: Mendes I. Cohen; Mrs. Harriet Cohen Coale

Selected Reference: Andrew Oliver, Jr., *Beyond the Shores of Tripoli, American Archaeology in the Eastern Mediterranean 1789–1879* (exh. cat.), Fogg Art Museum (Cambridge, Mass., 1979–80).

W. R. J.

20

CHARLES JAMES MADISON EATON   (1807–93)

Baltimore

C. J. M. Eaton was born in North Carolina to parents who had migrated from New England. He came to Baltimore as a young man, entered a merchant house, and by the age of thirty-three, had amassed a fortune sufficient to retire and devote himself to cultural pursuits. In his travels during the 1840s, Eaton visited London, where he was befriended by the prominent banker from Massachusetts and Baltimore, George Peabody.

In Baltimore, Eaton was a founder of the Mercantile Library Association and played a significant role, together with the businessman Osmond Tiffany, in raising funds to erect the Athenaeum Building, which housed The Maryland Historical Society.

Eaton was one of the principal lenders to the Society's first exhibitions. In 1849, his entries included a painting of Saint Jerome (said to be by Paul Delaroche), two Roman views by "Van Vittelli," and two landscapes by the American painters T. W. Whittridge and C. L. Brown. Eaton's contributions were particularly numerous in 1853 and included more than eighteen pictures by Old Masters, contemporary European artists, and American painters.

Later in life, Eaton was fully engrossed in The Peabody Institute. He had been chosen by its founder to serve as one of the original trustees, and presided over the board of trustees from 1878 until his death, fifteen years later. At that time, Eaton's next of kin, two nieces, donated the Eaton collection to the Institute. The collection included eighty-one paintings, sixty-two watercolors, many drawings (including those from the Robert Gilmor, Jr., collection), portrait miniatures, and a dozen bronzes initially thought to be by A. L. Barye but later identified as the works of Christophe Fratin.

Suggestions for Further Reading: "The Death of Charles J. M. Eaton," *The Baltimore Sun* (16 January 1893), 8; "Mr. Charles J. M. Eaton Dead," *The Baltimore American* (15 January 1893), 8.

W. R. J.

CHRISTOPHE FRATIN
French, 1800–64
21 *Panther and Cubs Stalking an African Native*
    (1834)
Bronze

Height: 8 ½ inches
Lent by The Peabody Institute of the City of Baltimore; on indefinite loan to The Baltimore Museum of Art

After studying in his native Metz with C. A. Pioche, Fratin went to Paris to enroll in the studio of Géricault. His first entries in the Paris Salon, *Fermer, an English Thorough-*

bred and *Two Bulldogs Playing and a Greyhound,* were shown as wax models in 1831, the same year that his rival animalier, A. L. Barye, entered the *Tiger and Gavial.* Though Fratin never attained the fame of Barye, he received a number of government commissions and enjoyed a following in the United States and Great Britain. One of his largest compositions, *Two Eagles Guarding Their Prey,* can be seen in Central Park, New York; at the Great Exhibition of 1851, he was acclaimed the greatest animalier of his time. Many of Fratin's early works, cast in plaster by Susse Frères, have disappeared; he is therefore remembered for his small bronzes, cast by the firm of E. Quesnel.

In Baltimore, William T. Walters placed one of Fratin's large statues of a dog outside his country residence, "Saint Mary's," and Charles J. M. Eaton acquired a dozen examples of the artist's smaller bronzes.

Signed and Dated: *Fratin/1834*

Provenance: Charles J. M. Eaton

——————————————— *W. R. J.*

21

22

CHRISTOPHE FRATIN

22   *Lion Attacking an African Native*   (1834)
Bronze
Height: 9 ¾ inches
Lent by The Peabody Institute of the City of Baltimore; on indefinite loan to The Baltimore Museum of Art

Glenn Benge, citing this composition as an illustration of Fratin's indebtedness to Barye, compares the fallen native to the fallen assassin in Barye's plaster group in the Louvre, *Charles II Surprised in the Forest of Man* (Salon of 1833).

Signed and Dated: *Fratin Sc/1834*

Provenance: Charles J. M. Eaton

Selected Reference: Glenn Benge, "Christophe Fratin," in *The Romantics to Rodin* (exh. cat.) Los Angeles County Museum of Art (1980/81), 271.

——————————————— *W. R. J.*

THOMAS EDMONDSON   (1808–56)

Baltimore

During his brief period of activity, Dr. Thomas Edmondson was one of the most acquisitive collectors Baltimore has ever seen. Educated as a doctor of medicine at the University of Maryland, Edmondson's interests in the fine arts, literature, and horticulture must have vastly outweighed his scientific pursuits, for there is no record of his ever having practiced the profession of his training.

The dashing young collector was one of five children of Mary Cockbain (1783–1849) and Thomas Edmondson (1765–1836), a wealthy Baltimore merchant who had emigrated from Liverpool. In 1845, the younger Edmondson married Mary Howell (1822–53), the daughter of Susan E. Miles (1801–67) and John Brown Howell (1791–1855), a Baltimore shipping merchant. Dr. and Mrs. Edmondson had four children—Mary, Alice, Henry, and Emma.

The doctor's interest in the fine arts must have been encouraged early in his life, and was perhaps supported financially by a large inheritance from his bachelor uncle, Isaac Edmondson (1770–1822). The first evidence of this interest is a reply from John James Audubon, dated 1833 (collection of The Maryland Historical Society, Baltimore), regarding Edmondson's inquiry as to the manner in which Audubon's *Birds of America* was being printed and distributed. Edmondson was but twenty-five years old at the time. Horticulture, too, was one of the collector's early interests, which mixed with that in the fine arts in 1834, when Edmondson commissioned the artist Nicolino Calyo to portray the Edmondson estate, "Harlem" (collection of the Henry Francis du Pont Winterthur Museum), in a painting that devoted particular attention and detail to the extensive gardens and greenhouse.

By the time of his early death at the age of forty-eight, the doctor's collection included more than two hundred paintings. He had been an important patron of local artists, commissioning several family portraits from Richard Caton Woodville, Michael Laty, Hugh Newell, Ernst Fischer, and Alfred Jacob Miller. These last three local painters were obvious favorites of Edmondson, for—in addition to the portraits—he owned ten works by Newell, eleven by Miller, and thirty-two by Fischer. Edmondson was thus Fischer's chief patron.

The Edmondson collection included European paintings, such as *Tame Ducks* by Hondecoeter, *Spanish Dogs* by Richard Ansdale, and many copies of Old Masters' works, but its strength was in works by local contemporary artists. Other American artists were also represented; Edmondson owned a still life by the "elder" Peale; the immense painting, *Virginia Wedding,* by William Tyler Ranney, and a sea piece by Thomas Birch. He also owned more than 150 engravings, most of which are known today only by their titles: *Venice, View of Baltimore Street, Baltimore in 1752, Naples, Landscape, Returning from Ascot, Foxhunting* (a set of four), *Crucifixion, Nature* (by Sir T. Lawrence), and *Village Festival* (by Wouwerman), as well as Benjamin West's portraits.

Books were also of tremendous interest to Edmondson; his was one of the greatest Baltimore libraries of the day. Included in this collection were many important contemporary works and volumes dating before the nineteenth century. After Edmondson's death, the library was auctioned off, the sale including more than eight hundred lots netting $5,722—the top price being $750 for Audubon's *Birds of America.*

Edmondson's third major interest was in his gardens and plants. Within weeks of his death, the greenhouses were emptied and sold at auction. The sale consisted of 236 lots, most with examples of one plant type—such as lot number 234, which included "1088 Azalia [*sic*] Seedlings in Pots." The following spring, another sale was conducted to dispose of Edmondson's fancy lawn plants and garden equipment. Thus, within six months of his death, the largest collection of the former president of the Horticultural Society had been dispersed.

Edmondson's interests in the fine arts were not limited to collecting. In 1848, he was active in arranging The Maryland Historical Society's first annual exhibition; the following year, he became a member of its Gallery Committee; and until his death, he remained active as both an advisor and a lender to the Society's exhibitions.

At the time of Edmondson's death, more than 120 works from his collection were placed on deposit with The Maryland Historical Society, until his children, then minors, came of age. Records indicate that in 1874 the estate was finally divided among the heirs, and each of them received lots of approximately seventy paintings and engravings. In March of that year, the library was dispersed, and in May, one heir's lot of fine arts was sold at auction. The sale included 46 paintings and 23 engravings, including a *Landscape* by A. J. Miller, the *Ship at Sea* by Thomas Birch, and the *View off the Coast of Holland* by van Ensrich. Edmondson's other heirs were among the active buyers.

Today, paintings from Edmondson's collection can be found in The Maryland Historical Society, The Baltimore Museum of Art, the Henry F. Du Pont Winterthur Museum, and private collections. The largest single group of paintings remaining together, about a dozen, survive in England, in the possession of a great-great-granddaughter.

Suggestions for Further Reading: Thomas Edmondson, *Catalogue of a . . . Collection of Lawn Plants . . .* (Baltimore, 1857); *Catalogue of a Splendid Collection of Books . . .* (Baltimore, 1870); *Catalogue of . . . Green House Plants . . . to be sold by public auction* (Baltimore, 1857); *List of Paintings belonging to the Estate of Dr. Edmondson . . . January 1859.* Archives of The Maryland Historical Society (MS 2008); *Important Art Sale of Rare and Valuable Oil Paintings and Engravings . . .* (Baltimore, 1874); Maryland Historical Society Catalogues of Exhibitions (1848–1908); Dr. J. Hall Pleasants, *Studies in Maryland Painting,* Curatorial Offices of The Maryland Historical Society.

—— *S. T. C.*

NICOLINO CALYO
Italian-American, 1799–1884
23 *Fairmount Park, Balloon Ascension of 1834*
(1834)
Gouache
16 ⅝ x 30 inches
Lent by The Maryland Historical Society; Gift from the Estate of Miss Ethel Hough, Miss Anne Hough, and Miss Mary Hough

Calyo left his native Naples in about 1822 and embarked on travels that brought him to Baltimore in 1834. He remained in Baltimore until late the following year, when he departed for New York. There are four extant gouaches associated with Calyo's Baltimore sojourn: this work and a view of Dr. Edmondson's estate, "Harlem," now in the Winterthur Museum (both executed

while in Baltimore); a *View of the Port of Baltimore,* painted in 1836, in the Baltimore Museum of Art, and a *View of Baltimore from Federal Hill,* dated 1837.

Ballooning at Fairmount Park was very much in vogue during the summer of 1834. *Niles' Weekly Register* records three ascents: that of Mr. Mills on 3 May, one of Mr. Woodall and a young lady on 21 June, and

23

24

another of Mr. Parker and a passenger on 9 August.

Discernible to the viewer looking at Baltimore from the east are the shot towers, the Cathedral, the Washington Monument, and the Federal Hill Observatory.

Signed: (at lower left): *N. Calyo f/D'apres/natura*

Provenance: Dr. Thomas Edmondson; Mrs. Samuel Johnson Hough; the Misses Hough.

——————————————— *W.R.J.*

ERNST GEORG FISCHER
German-American, 1815–74
24 *Portrait of a Lady/Girl with Roses—Parlor of "Harlem"* *(1854)*
Oil on canvas
24 ½ x 20 inches
Lent anonymously

The traditional identification of the young lady in this interior as one of Dr. Edmondson's three daughters—Mary (b.1846), Alice (b.1849), or Emma (b.1851)—is at variance with the actual ages of the three girls at the time of Fischer's activity in Baltimore (from about 1848 to about 1854). Similar discrepancies in age appear in Fischer's two group portraits thought to represent the Edmondsons at "Harlem," their country estate: *Country Life* (in The

Maryland Historical Society) and *Dr. Edmondson and His Family* (in The Baltimore Museum of Art). The subject in this portrait most closely resembles the lady identified as Mrs. Edmondson (1822–52) in The Maryland Historical Society's picture.

Ernst Georg Fischer, a native of Coburg, Germany, was trained in Germany and at Antwerp and Paris before coming to the United States. Thirty of his paintings from the estate of Dr. Edmondson, his principal patron, were exhibited at The Maryland Historical Society in 1858.

Signed: (at lower right): *E Fischer/Baltimore 1854*

Provenance: Dr. Thomas Edmondson; Mrs. Samuel Johnson Hough; the Misses Hough; Norton Asner

——————————————— *W.R.J.*

THE LEE COLLECTION OF "NEEDWOOD"   (early 19th century)
Frederick County

A little-known but interesting collection of Italian and northern European paintings was assembled during the first half of the nineteenth century at "Needwood," the Lee family residence in the Middletown Valley, Frederick County. The collection, which included pictures once attributed to Orcagna, Giovanni Tosicani, Parmigianino, Hugo van der Goes, Charles Le Brun, and Johann Rottenhammer, was donated in 1947 to Mount Saint Mary's College, Emmitsburg, by Dr. Thomas S. Lee in memory of his father, Dr. Charles Carroll Lee (1839–93).

"Needwood," built in 1808, was the home of Thomas Sim Lee (1745–1819), a zealous patriot and supporter of George Washington, and governor of Maryland for two terms. With his marriage to Mary Digges, Thomas Sim Lee converted to Roman Catholicism. One of his sons, John Lee (1788–1871), who served as a Democratic congressman from 1823 to 1825, married Harriet Carroll, a daughter of Charles Carroll of Carrollton. Their son, Charles Carroll Lee, was raised at "Needwood" and graduated from Mount Saint Mary's College in 1856. After training in medicine at the University of Pennsylvania and serving as a surgeon in the Union Army, Charles Carroll Lee moved to New York to practice medicine.

Although this Dr. Lee was a patron of the arts and acquired works by his former classmates at Mount Saint Mary's (including John La Farge and Augustus Saint-Gaudens), he is thought to have inherited the early pictures from his family. Both the Parmigianino and the Rottenhammer were listed as family pictures, and a picture attributed to Francesco Francia is known to have been acquired by his aunt, Mrs. Robert Goodloe Harper, who went to Europe on a grand tour in 1819/20.

Suggestions for Further Reading: Mary Fisher, "First Families of Maryland," *The Baltimore Post* (7 February 1933), 9; Outerbridge Horsey, "Governor Thomas Sim Lee," *The Society of the Lees of Virginia* (May 1974); Kelly Fitzpatrick, "The Mount's Artistic Heritage," *Mount Saint Mary's Mountaineer Briefing* 21, 3(1983):18–19.

——— *W. R. J.*

COPY AFTER FRANCESCO MAZZOLA
(or Mazzuoli), known as IL PARMIGIANINO
Italian, 1503–40
25 *Madonna and Child with Saint Zacharias, the Magdalen, and the Infant Saint John*
Oil on panel
28 ¾ x 22 ¼ inches
Lent by Mount Saint Mary's College, Emmitsburg; Given by Thomas Sim Lee in memory of his father, Charles Carroll Lee, 1947

Profoundly influenced by Correggio and the accomplishments of Raphael and Michelangelo, Parmigianino became one of the leading exponents of Mannerism. The extremely refined, almost decorative elegance of his figures and the intense, somewhat acidic colors typical of his works make them paradigms of the abstract ideals of beauty that characterize this style. A prolific draftsman and graphic artist, Parmigianino exerted an international influence. During his last years, he neglected art in favor of alchemy, and his efforts to solidify mercury may have contributed to his early death.

Aside from being slightly cropped on the right, the Lee panel replicates the master's original composition painted in about 1530 for a Bolognese patron, Bonafazio Gozzadini, which is now in the Uffizi, Florence. The work exhibits those qualities that earned Parmigianino the praise of Vasari, who admired his "power of making beautiful landscapes" and the "singular grace with which he endowed his figures." In his discussion of the Uffizi panel, Freedberg argues that the Michelangelesque figure of Zacharias in the foreground serves as an illusionistic device leading the viewer into the composition, which, with its idealized figures and its shimmering, ethereal atmosphere, supports Copertini's suggestion that this devotional image be interpreted as the "Vision of Zacharias," the father of John the Baptist (G. Copertini, *Il Parmigianino*, Parma, 1932, 1:120).

In the early nineteenth century, when this painting was acquired, Parmigianino's work was thought to approach the pinnacle of accomplishments achieved by Raphael— as Vasari reports, Parmigianino's "own beautiful work and graceful manners led to the saying that the spirit of Raphael had passed into him." The painting was engraved twice by Bonasone (Bartsch XV.124.54 and .55), and its popularity is further attested by the ten copies and variants listed by Freedberg. Another copy was recently offered by Christie's, New York, 10 January 1980, lot 5.

Provenance: John Lee, Charles Carroll Lee, Thomas Sim Lee

Selected References: Sydney Freedberg, *Parmigianino* (Cambridge, Mass., 1950), 82–83, 182–84; Giorgio Vasari, *Lives . . .*, trans. A. B. Hinds, 4 vols. (London, n.d.), 3:6–14.

——————————————————————————————————— *B. B.*

JOHAN ROTTENHAMMER
German, 1564–1625
26 *Resurrection*
Oil on copper
14 ⅞ x 11 ⅟₁₆ inches
Lent by Mount Saint Mary's College, Emmitsburg; Given by Thomas Sim Lee in memory of his father, Charles Carroll Lee, 1947

After training in Germany, Rottenhammer traveled to Rome, where he collaborated with Jan Brueghel the Elder and Paul Bril, painting figures in their fanciful landscapes. After working in Venice from 1596 to 1606, he returned to Germany and worked at Schloss Bückeburg (1609–13) before settling in Augsburg. Rottenhammer's composition·is derived from the *Resurrection* in the church of San Francesco della Vigna, Venice, a fresco attributed to Paolo Veronese (T. Pignatti, *Veronese*, 2 vols., Venice, 1976, 1:213, no.A329, fig.1002). The preciosity of Rottenhammer's technique, combined with his elegant draftsmanship and the meticulous detail of his religious, mythological, and allegorical compositions, appealed to notable patrons of late Mannerist art, such as the emperor Rudolph II.

Provenance: John Lee, Charles Carroll Lee, Thomas Sim Lee, Mount Saint Mary's College

——————————————————————— *B. B.*

25

26

JAMES HOWARD McHENRY   (1820–88)

Pikesville

James Howard McHenry is remembered as an individual who traveled extensively and mastered several languages. His obituary also noted "his refined taste" and "the many beautiful objects of art which adorn[ed] his mansion." As was characteristic of the many collectors of his time, McHenry's taste was for replicas of Old Master paintings, which he probably acquired as souvenirs of his trips abroad, as well as for original works by the esteemed artists, which occasionally became available. McHenry's loans to the 1848 exhibition of The Maryland Historical Society included watercolor copies by "Roster" of Guido Reni's *Cleopatra* (no. 268), Murillo's *Madonna and Infant Christ* (no. 269), Titian's *Flora* (no. 270), and Hiram Powers' sketch of the *Greek Slave* (no. 314), and two marble busts (nos. 317 and 318).

The collector was the son of Colonel John McHenry and Juliana Elizabeth Howard. His paternal grandfather, James McHenry, after whom the Baltimore fort is named, served as Lafayette's chief of staff and as Secretary of War, while his maternal grandfather was none other than Colonel John Eager Howard, the Revolutionary War hero. Orphaned at age two, McHenry was placed in the charge of an uncle, Charles Howard, who educated him at a school in Geneva and at Princeton University. He studied law at Harvard and practiced his profession in Baltimore. McHenry was also a gentleman-farmer noted for his exceptional herds of Devon and Jersey cattle, which he maintained at his country estate, "Sudbrook," near Pikesville, north of Baltimore.

Suggestion for Further Reading: "Death of Mr. James Howard McHenry," *Baltimore American* (26 September 1888), 4.

—*W.R.J.*

HIRAM POWERS
American, 1805–73
27 *Proserpine*
Marble
Height: 22 inches
Lent by The Maryland Historical Society; Gift of Mr.
James McHenry, Priscilla McHenry Farnsworth,
and Mrs. Joseph France

After a successful career as a portraitist in Washington, Powers embarked for Europe with his family in 1837 and opened a studio in Florence. Taking advantage of the readily available, fine marble and the many artisans capable of transposing his compositions from plaster to stone, Powers quickly established himself in Italy. In addition to executing portraits of American tourists, he sought to produce idealized, Classical figures. With his *Greek Slave,* shown in the Great Exhibition in London in 1851, Powers acquired international renown. One of his most pop-

ular works was the bust of Proserpine, first produced in 1839/40 and subsequently replicated more than a hundred times. In this version, the daughter of Demeter, goddess of agriculture, is shown with a strand of wheat in her hair and a severe, foliate border around her base. In other versions, she is shown emerging from a base exuberantly adorned with acanthus leaves.

McHenry acquired two marble busts by Powers in the course of his travels—this *Proserpine* and a replica of the *Greek Slave,* which he also lent to The Maryland Historical Society in 1848.

Signed: (on reverse): *H POWERS SCULP*

Provenance: Purchased by James Howard McHenry

Selected Exhibition: "First annual exhibition of The Maryland Historical Society," Baltimore, 1848, no. 318

———— *W.R.J.*

27

JOHN W. McCOY   (1821–89)
Baltimore

Among Baltimore's "parlor collections" of the early 1880s noted by Edward Strahan, was that of John W. McCoy. Unlike so many of his contemporaries, McCoy never became fully enamored of fashionable European painting, but remained a staunch patron of local talent, particularly of the sculptor William H. Rinehart and the painters Thomas Hovenden, Arthur Quartley, and Hugh Bolton Jones.

Throughout his career, John W. McCoy was an exceptionally civic-minded individual and an active member of the community. After graduating from Baltimore City College and the University of Maryland, he worked as an editorial writer for a weekly magazine and served as an officer of the Allston Club, a private organization dedicated to furthering art and literature. In 1859, McCoy took control of two North Carolina mining companies with offices in Baltimore, and during the course of the Civil War he managed with remarkable ingenuity to keep these concerns in operation. In 1865, he became a principal partner of William T. Walters & Company, a wholesale liquor house in Baltimore. A man of apparently boundless energy, McCoy became one of the first members of the Baltimore Association for Improvement of the Condition of the Poor, serving the charity as a volunteer field officer. He was also an administrator for the Spring Grove State Insane Asylum. Although he did not resign from the liquor business until 1880, McCoy also found time to run the *Daily Evening Bulletin*, a journal he had helped to found four years earlier.

After 1881, McCoy was listed in the city directories merely as the president of the Mercantile Library Association, a private library started in 1839 that had fallen on bad times and which might have closed without McCoy's intervention. The association's librarian, John W. M. Lee, was also employed by McCoy, whose library was said to be without equal locally in the fields of English and American history, natural science, travel, illustrated topography, and engraved reproductions.

John W. McCoy bequeathed his books and the bulk of his estate to The Johns Hopkins University. His art collection—including sixty-nine pictures, mostly by American artists, and five pieces of sculpture—was given to The Peabody Institute in two lots, one at the time of his death and the other in 1908, following the closing of the Athenaeum Club.

Suggestions for Further Reading: J. Thomas Scharf, *History of Baltimore City and County* (Philadelphia, 1881), 660–62; Peabody Institute Gallery of Art, *List of Works on Exhibition, October, 1910* (Baltimore, 1910).

———*W.R.J.*

28 *COMPILATION OF TEXTS ON "THE SECRETS OF WOMEN"*
German (Saxon), late 16th century
Manuscript on paper, contemporary blind-stamped binding
12 x 8 inches
Lent by the Special Collections Division of the Milton S. Eisenhower Library, The Johns Hopkins University (MS 38,066)

In light of the taste of his time, John W. McCoy displayed exceptional acumen in acquiring this unillustrated German Renaissance manuscript. The contents and ornamented binding are both fine examples of the humanistic interests prevailing in Germany during the post-Reformation era. The text, comprising in large part *De secretis mulierum,* ascribed to Albertus Magnus at the time of transcription, enjoyed particular popularity in the later sixteenth century. (In Frankfurt alone, three editions of German translations from the Latin were issued between 1581 and 1592).

The vogue indubitably accounts for the production of this manuscript. Its special appeal is enhanced by a blind-stamped, unstained leather binding ornamented with individual decorative tools, as well as figural rolls representative of the type of imagery favored by German bibliophiles of the time. An airy border of stylized, foliate arabesques indicative of French influence surrounds a more typically German band of female personifications of Justice, Faith, Charity, and wifely virtue in the guise of Lucretia. Shown half-length in contemporary gowns with puff-and-slash sleeves, these figures appear above framed, identifying inscriptions. A narrower, inner foliate band contains a repeat of three male heads more cryptically labeled *CARO[LUS]* (Emperor Charles V), *SOLI* (? a reference to the sun, Solinus, or possibly Solomon), and *OCDA [? VIANUS]* (perhaps Emperor Octavian Augustus). In the central panel of the upper cover is an elaborate coat of arms, which is repeated on a bookplate dated 1594. Belonging to an elector of Saxony, who may in fact have commissioned the volume, the armorial device adds distinc-

29

ASHER BROWN DURAND
American, 1796–1886

29 *Landscape, A Study from Nature* (1850s)
Oil on canvas
24 x 18 ¼ inches
Lent by The Peabody Institute of the City of Bal-
timore; on indefinite loan to The Baltimore
Museum of Art

Durand, seeking to avoid conventionality in his painting, emphasized the primacy of nature rather than artistic tradition as his instructor. He saw a special role for the American landscape painter who, being "free from academic or other restraints by virtue of his position," would, "in accordance with the principle of self-government, boldly originate a high and independent style, based on his native resources" (Asher B. Durand, "Letter 2," of 17 January 1855, *The Crayon,* 1:3, 35). As a consequence, Durand frequently painted out-of-doors, one of the earliest American artists to do so.

Although remembered principally as a patron of local painters, John W. McCoy occasionally acquired works by the leading artists of his time, including this landscape by the president of the National Academy of Design.

Signed: (at lower right): *A. B. Durand*

Provenance: John W. McCoy; The Peabody Institute

Selected Exhibition: "American Masterpieces of the Peabody Art Collection," The Peabody Institute of The Johns Hopkins University, 1983,7

28

tion to this binding, which was produced under the influence of the master craftsman Jakob Krause (d.1585), known to have worked in Dresden under the special pat-ronage of Augustus I, elector of Saxony.

Provenance: Baron Christopher of Wolkenstein, armorial en-graved bookplate dated 1594; John W. McCoy, Baltimore; be-queathed to The Johns Hopkins University

Selected References: De Ricci, *Census,* 1:753, no.3; cf. Ilse Schunke, *Studien zum Bilderschmuck der Deutschen Renais-sance-Einbände* (Wiesbaden, 1959), and *Leben und Werk Jakob Krauses* (Leipzig, n.d.)

———————————————— *L.M.C.R.*

———————————————— *W.R.J.*

30

EPHRAIM KEYSER
American, 1850–1937
30 *John W. McCoy* (1880)
Marble
Height: 2 ½ inches
Lent by The Peabody Institute of the City of Baltimore

One of Baltimore's most successful sculptors at the turn of the century, Keyser is remembered chiefly for his marble *Psyche* (1877) in the Cincinnati Art Museum, his statue of General Baron de Kalb (1886) in Annapolis, and his numerous portrait busts, including those of Sidney Lanier, Johns Hopkins, and John W. McCoy.

In Baltimore, he trained at the Maryland Institute and under A. J. Volk at the Maryland Academy of Art. Subsequently, he went to Germany to study with Max Widnmann at the Munich Academy (1872–76) and with Albert Wolff at the Berlin Academy (1877).

Upon his return to America, Keyser served as an instructor of modeling at the Maryland Institute from 1892 until 1923 and was appointed director of the Rinehart School of Sculpture in 1898.

Early guides to Baltimore list this work as being exhibited in The Peabody Institute's Gallery of Sculpture.

Inscription: (on socle): *John W. McCoy/born April 2, 1821*

Signed: *E. Keyser fec./Balto./1880*

Selected Reference: Ulrich Thieme and Felix Becker, *Allgemeines Lexikon der Bildenden Künstler* (Leipzig, 1927), 20:236.

——————————————————— *W. R. J.*

ROBERT C. HALL   (1830–1908)
Baltimore

Among the local collectors of contemporary American art during the second half of the nineteenth century was Robert C. Hall, a native of Somerset County, Maryland. Orphaned at the age of fifteen, he received instruction in Classics from a Unitarian minister, but was otherwise self-educated. He married in about 1858 and found employment in New York at the Gillette Tea Company. With the outbreak of the Civil War, Hall, a secessionist sympathizer, returned to Maryland, intending to volunteer for military service. Given the course of events, he instead joined an older brother, John, in establishing a wholesale coal business, Hall Brothers and Company, with offices at 36 South Holliday Street. The business prospered, and Hall was able to purchase two residences, a town house at 1014 Madison Avenue and a country house on York Road.

An inventory of pictures in Hall's estate included works by such local talents as A. J. H. Way, H. Bolton Jones, and A. Quartley; a few by other American artists, such as T. Hovenden and A. T. Bricher; and a number of paintings by lesser-known Europeans, among them P. Seignac, and several identified as Wagner, Scharlia, Louts, etc. A highlight of the collection was the painting, *In Hoc Signo Vinces (La Vendée, 1793),* which Hovenden had valued at $3,000 when he exhibited it at the National Academy of Design's 1881 exhibition.

Suggestion for Further Reading: Richard H. Randall, Jr., "Sunset on the Newburyport Marshes," *Bulletin of The Walters Art Gallery* 30, 4 (January 1978).

——— *W. R. J.*

MARTIN JOHNSON HEADE
American, 1819–1904
31 *Sunset on the Newburyport Marshes* (1862)
Oil on canvas
25 ¹/₁₆ x 50 inches
The Walters Art Gallery (37.2531); Gift of Dr. Alan C. Woods, Jr., 1976

Although Heade had painted some landscapes previously, he only discovered the subject to be his true métier in 1859, when he rented a studio in New York and became acquainted with members of the Hudson River School, especially Frederick E. Church, who became his lifelong friend. Thereafter,

Heade's oeuvre falls into three major categories: landscapes, including views of marshes, beaches, and jungles; still lifes, usually of roses and magnolias; and pictures of hummingbirds, often with orchids. Heade's landscapes are regarded as archetypal examples of "luminism," a uniquely

American style prevalent about 1870–75.

Painted in 1862, *Sunset on the New-buryport Marshes* is among the first in the series of marshscapes with stacks of salt hay, scenes that Heade continued to produce during the remainder of his career. More than one hundred examples survive, illustrating the slow decline of the artist's style as his compositions and brushwork became looser, beginning in the 1870s. Like Claude Monet's haystacks, Heade's marshscapes demonstrate the artist's abiding concern with the effects of light on the same subject under a variety of atmospheric conditions. His subtly varied combinations of the same elements—haystacks, rivers, and atmosphere—suggest an underlying effort to formulate a "perfect" composition.

31

Provenance: Robert C. Hall, Baltimore; Dr. Alan C. Woods, Jr.

Selected References: R. H. Randall, Jr., "Sunset on the New-buryport Marshes," *Bulletin of The Walters Art Gallery* 30, 4 (January 1978); National Gallery of Art, *American Light: The Luminist Movement, 1850–1875* (Washington, DC, 1980), 83, fig. 76.

——————————————— *B. B.*

ALFRED THOMPSON BRICHER
American, 1837–1908
32 *Riverview* (1880s)
Oil on canvas
12 ¹³⁄₁₆ x 24 ¹⁄₁₆ inches
The Walters Art Gallery (37.2525)

Bricher, a landscape and marine painter, enjoyed a moderate success in his long career, producing works that frequently echoed the endeavors of his colleagues, M. J. Heade and Fitz Hugh Lane. He was born in Portsmouth, New Hampshire, and was raised in Newburyport, Massachusetts, spending the first portion of his career based in Boston and sketching throughout New England. In 1868 he moved to New York, but continued to return in the summers to his New England haunts.

Though labeled "Riverview," this composition most closely resembles his shoreline views of Lake George. He first sketched at that site in 1867 and, in the mid-1880s, produced several paintings showing rowboats and figures with parasols (see "Alfred Thompson Bricher, 1837–1908," Indianapolis Museum of Art and George Walter Vincent Smith Art Museum ⟨1973/74⟩, nos. 60–61).

Signed: (at lower left): *A. T. Bricher*

Provenance: Robert C. Hall; Mrs. Daisy W. Woods

——————————————— *W. R. J.*

J. STRICKER JENKINS   (1831–78)
Baltimore

Colonel J. Stricker Jenkins might have become Maryland's principal collector of contemporary European painting, had ill health not compelled him to sell his collection two years before his death at the age of forty-seven.

John Stricker Jenkins was the son of Hugh Jenkins (1798⟨?⟩–1863), of Waterford, Ireland, who immigrated to Baltimore and established a prosperous import house specializing in Brazilian coffee. The fine arts were apparently of interest to the senior Jenkins, for he is listed among the patrons of J. J. Audubon and was the owner of a landscape by J. F. Cropsey, which was exhibited in 1849 at The Maryland Historical Society's second annual exhibition.

J. Stricker Jenkins entered his father's business in 1850, married Clara V. Vanderwoort of New York in 1855, and by the following year had begun to acquire pictures by American artists. Among his early acquisitions were a still life and three studies, including a copy after Raphael, commissioned from A. J. Miller in 1856–57. In the course of the following decade, Jenkins purchased works at a phenomenal pace, extending his interests to European art. His loans to The Maryland Historical Society in 1868 included pictures by the Americans F. E. Church, J. F. Kensett, S. R. Gifford, G. A. Baker, and G. H. Boughton, as well as a *Romeo and Juliet* by the popular French figurative painter, C. F. Jalabert, and a *Trooper in the Snow* by the Austrian, A. Schreyer.

Jenkins apparently adopted the practice of receiving visitors to his residence at 176 North Charles Street, and in 1870 he published a catalogue of the collection, listing forty-seven American paintings and drawings, forty-five European pictures, four statues, and a large enameled vase. Although Jenkins' taste appears to have been catholic for the period, the catalogue reflects his preference for landscapes by American painters and figurative and genre works by the Europeans. The chef d'oeuvre was undoubtedly W. A. Bouguereau's *Art and Literature.*

The sale of the Jenkins collection at Clinton Hall in New York, on 2 and 3 May 1876, realized a somewhat disappointing sum of $66,000, the highest prices being paid for A. Schreyer's *Retreat* and C. Delort's *The Proclamation.* Bouguereau's *Art and Literature,* failing to attain a reserve, was withdrawn from the sale.

In addition to his business and artistic interests, Jenkins is remembered as one of the six founders of Baltimore's Fifth Regiment Infantry, an organization in which he served as Lieutenant Colonel from 1867 to 1871 and as Colonel from 1871 until 1876, when illness forced him to resign from public life.

Suggestions for Further Reading: *Baltimore American* (9 April 1978); George A Meakins, *Fifth Regiment Infantry* (Baltimore, 1899), 8, 25–28, 82; Robinson C. Watters, "Audubon and His Baltimore Patrons," *Maryland Historical Magazine* 34(1939):138–43 [Hugh Jenkins].

—— *W. R. J.*

WILLIAM-ADOLPHE BOUGUEREAU
French, 1825–1905
33 *Art and Literature* (1867)
Oil on canvas
78 ¾ x 42 ½ inches
Lent by the Arnot Art Museum, Elmira

In the course of the Third Republic, Bouguereau achieved an international reputation as a figurative painter and as a professor at the Ecole des Beaux-Arts. His style of painting owed much to his sojourn in Italy (from 1850 to 1854) where he was particularly drawn to the works of Giotto and Raphael.

Among Bouguereau's first American patrons was J. Stricker Jenkins, who commissioned this allegorical painting through the New York dealer, Samuel P. Avery, with the Baltimore expatriate George A. Lucas serving as an intermediary in Paris. For this commission Bouguereau was said to have

> expressed unusual delight to his American patron for a chance to give a loose to his classical feeling and idealism in a kind of theme which the dealers, enamored of his accomplished peasant-girls, seldom allowed him to attempt . . .
>
> (Strahan, 3:76)

According to Lucas, the painting was ordered in January 1866, and was completed by December 1867.

Art and Literature exemplifies Bouguereau's mature style in its high finish, harmonious colors, and the majestic grace of its idealized figures.

Provenance: Colonel J. Stricker Jenkins, Baltimore, Sale, Clinton Hall, New York, 2 and 3 May 1876, (bought in); E. Walter, New York, 1881; Henry Johnston, 1893; E. M. Harris, Providence, Rhode Island, Sale; American Art Association, New York, 14 April 1899, lot 160, $1,700 to Jules Oehme; Sale no.3939, Sotheby Parke-Bernet, New York, 14 January 1977, lot 191

Selected References: *Catalogue of Paintings and Other Works of Art Belonging to J. Stricker Jenkins, no. 187, N. Charles Street,* (Baltimore, 1870), no.12; Strahan, *The Art Treasures of America,* 3 vols. (Philadelphia, n.d.), 3:76–77, ill.; *The Diary of George A. Lucas: An American Art Agent in Paris, 1857—1909,* transcribed with an introduction by Lilian M. C. Randall, 2 vols. (Princeton, 1979), 2:206, 212, 221, 234, 251, 256, 258, 262.

———————————————————————————————————— *B. B.*

33

WILLIAM H. CRIM   (1845–1902)

Baltimore

Marylanders have yet to witness an auction rivaling that held in Baltimore in April 1903, to liquidate the collection of Dr. Crim. For ten days, 22 April to 4 May, the public flocked to the Fourth Regiment Armory to bid or merely to gape as 2,941 items were dispersed, realizing a sum of $70,000. The press reported the proceedings daily, noting how "local society folk, collectors and dealers" contended "good naturedly against out-of-town curio hunters."

The doctor who had assembled this collection was a native of Loudon County, Virginia. After completing a collegiate course in Gettysburg, William Crim began the study of medicine in a private office in Lovettsville, Virginia. Later, he matriculated at the University of Maryland, completing his training in 1870 with a year's residency at University Hospital.

From all reports, it may be inferred that Crim was a remarkably energetic individual. In addition to practicing medicine in Baltimore as a surgeon and physician, he conducted private classes in medical instruction. He also was active in the Fifth Regiment Infantry, serving as Captain and Assistant Surgeon from 1872 to 1880, and subsequently as Major and Surgeon. Until age disqualified him at the time of the Spanish-American War, Crim participated in all of the regiment's campaigns, acting on occasion as its arbiter in artistic matters; he designed the fasces-shaped floral arrangement for the dedication of A. Merciés statue of General Lee in Richmond in May 1890.

Although Crim's taste as a collector was eclectic, he excelled in the field of decorative arts, particularly those pertaining to America. Historical associations and patriotic sentiment, rather than purely aesthetic considerations, seem often to have determined the course of his collecting. Among the items noted by the press at the liquidation sale were the first Bowie knife, the Scottish ram's horn snuffbox from the office of David Barnum of Barnum's Hotel, and the "Lafayette Bed" used by the general on his visit to the Old Fountain Inn in 1825. The highest price at the auction, however, was $8,000, paid by a New York dealer acting on behalf of the Gould family, for eight armchairs thought to have been from the shop of Thomas Chippendale, which formerly had been in the possession of Francis Scott Key. Even if his collection represents the results of zeal rather than aesthetic discernment, Crim must still be acknowledged as Maryland's pioneer collector in the field of the American arts.

Suggestions for Further Reading: *The Biographical Cyclopedia of Representative Men of Maryland and the District of Columbia* (Baltimore, 1879), 657; George A. Meekins, *Fifth Regiment Infantry* (Baltimore, 1899), 11, 131, 143, 159, 222, 297, 303; E. F. Cordell, M.D., *The Medical Annals of Maryland, 1799–1899* (Baltimore, 1903), 366.

———————————————————————————————————————*W. R. J.*

---

34   SIDE CHAIR
American (Maryland),   1770–90
Cherry wood with the seat frame in yellow pine
Height: 35 ¾ inches
Lent by The Maryland Historical Society, The Dr.
     Michael and Marie Abrams Memorial Fund

This chair, which is similar to one originally used in "Trentham," the Craddock family residence in the Greenspring Valley, exemplifies a Maryland variation of the Philadelphia Chippendale style. The local artisan has simplified the form and given the chair its distinctive, elongated ears.

Provenance: Dr. William H. Crim Sale, 22 April 1903, lot 2476, $65: Dr. Michael Abrams

Selected Reference: Gregory R. Weidman, *Furniture in Maryland, The Collection of The Maryland Historical Society* (Baltimore, 1984).

———————————————————————————*W. R. J.*

REMBRANDT PEALE
American, 1778–1860
35   *Portrait of Dr. James Smith*
Oil on canvas
23 ½ x 19 ⅜ inches
Lent by The Baltimore Museum of Art; Bequest of
     Elise Agnus Daingerfield

According to a notation in the Crim Sale catalogue, this portrait of the physician from Elkton, Maryland (1771–1841), who was famous for his pioneering work in introducing smallpox vaccination to the country, was painted for the portrait gallery of Rembrandt Peale's Museum and Gallery of Paintings, which opened on Holliday Street in Baltimore in 1814.

Rembrandt Peale was active as the city's foremost portraitist from 1814 until 1822, when he withdrew to New York.

Provenance: Rembrandt Peale's Baltimore Museum; William H. Crim Sale, Fourth Regiment Armory, Baltimore, 1903, no. 782.

Selected Reference: Sona K. Johnston, *American Paintings, 1750–1900, from the Collection of the Baltimore Museum of Art* (Baltimore, 1983), 123–24, no. 101.

———————————————————————————*W. R. J.*

35

34

JOHN FRANKLIN GOUCHER   (1845–1922)
Baltimore

The famous Maryland educator, John Franklin Goucher, was born in Waynesburg, Pennsylvania, in 1845. His parents, Emily Townsend and John Goucher, a medical doctor, were devout Methodists. In his early youth, the younger Goucher decided to enter the ministry instead of following in his father's footsteps. Goucher spent his boyhood in Pittsburgh and then went to Dickinson College, where he received his B.A. in 1868, his M.A. in 1872, his Doctor of Divinity in 1885, and finally, in 1889, a Doctor of Laws.

In 1869 Goucher went to Baltimore County on his first ministry, in which he supervised eight churches. There he met Mary Cecelia Fisher of Alto Dale in the Greenspring Valley, whom he married in 1877. This marriage made available the funds that Goucher was to use so creatively during the rest of his life in his many philanthropic projects. His great interest was in the foreign missions of the Church in Asia. He was an evangelistic Christian educator who believed that "evangelism without education faces fanaticism and reaction. Christian education is the most productive, the most prominent and far reaching form of evangelism." His lifelong interest in this work was rewarded when, in 1919, the emperor of Japan presented him with the third degree of the Order of the Rising Sun (Japan's highest civilian honor). In 1921, the president of China awarded Goucher the third degree of the Order of Chia Ho (likewise, the highest civilian honor of China).

Goucher is perhaps best known in Maryland for the very important part he played in the founding and launching of the college that bears his name. He was involved in the original creation of the institution in 1881, when the Baltimore Annual Conference of the Methodist Episcopal Church appointed a committee to consider the establishment of a seminary. Goucher made the first gift to the college in the form of land on St. Paul Street in Baltimore, and was instrumental in raising the funds that finally made the dream a reality. Goucher declined the invitation to become the first president of the new college because he did not want to limit his interests in education to one institution. He finally acquiesced to take the position in 1890, thus directing the course of the college in its formative years, until 1908.

Goucher, who was a frail child, was studious and broadly curious from the time of his youth. A friend once said of him that he "knew more about more things than any man I ever met." For instance, he enjoyed plants and took up a serious study of botany. Goucher collected many things and enjoyed showing his collections, kept in his two houses, to his guests. It is said that he once offered to unwrap one of his mummies for Dr. Lillian Welsh, the professor of physiology at Goucher College, who was a pioneer in insisting that physical education must be combined with the study of anatomy, physiology, and hygiene. He was an expert on early Methodist antiquities, manuscripts, and rare books, and built his collection of such material into one of the largest in the world.

A museum had been originated at the college in 1889 with the acquisition of a large collection of mineral specimens. In 1895, Goucher donated to this museum the high-quality, representative collection of antiquities that he had brought from Egypt. Goucher had acquired the ancient objects with the assistance of the colorful Emil Brugsch, a German Egyptologist and expert on the demotic script, who was assistant curator of the Cairo museum during the French regime. In 1881, Brugsch had launched the sudden and dramatic rescue of the cache of royal mummies that had been discovered and looted by the Rasul brothers, in the Theban cliffs near Luxor—the subject of the award-winning Egyptian movie, *The Night of Counting the Years.* Goucher also had contact with an even more famous antiquarian, Lord Elgin, who was responsible for bringing the Parthenon marbles to the British Museum. Goucher must have impressed him greatly, for after a morning spent discussing education, Lord Elgin presented the Goucher College library with a collection of rare works on India.

The range of Goucher's Egyptian collection represents a good cross section of Egyptian artifacts and well reflects the taste of a man who was devoted to education and to collecting.

Suggestion for Further Reading: Anna Heubeck Knipp and Thaddeus P. Thomas, *The History of Goucher College* (Baltimore, 1938), chs. 1–3.

——*J. V. C.*

---

36   PALETTE
Egyptian (Predynastic Period)
Slate
Greatest width: 5 ⅜ inches; Thickness: ⅛ inch
Lent by Goucher College, Baltimore (no. 29.6)

This palette in the shape of a plump fish was probably used to grind kohl for eye shadow. It is a fine example of an object characteristic of this early period. The fish is perforated

36

37

38

39

40

at the top of the back. The tail and the mouth area are chipped.

Provenance: Purchased by John Franklin Goucher, Egypt, 1889

————————————————————————*J. V. C.*

37   MINIATURE VESSEL
Egyptian, (Predynastic Period ⟨?⟩)
Black stone
Width (with lugs): 4 ⅜ inches; Height: ⅞ inch
Lent by Goucher College, Baltimore (no. 29.1)

This round dish, with an only slightly depressed interior, has four projecting lugs around the rim and a slightly offset base. The vessel probably imitates a grinding stone.

Provenance: Purchased by John Franklin Goucher, Egypt, 1889

————————————————————————*J. V. C.*

38   MORTAR AND PESTLE
Egyptian (Predynastic Period), 3000 B.C.
Gray and black conglomerate stone
Greatest diameter of vessel: 2 ⅛ inches; Height:
     1 ¼ inches; Height (of pestle): 1 ⅜ inches
Lent by Goucher College, Baltimore (no. 29.3)

This set was probably used to grind kohl for eye shadow. The shape of the mortar, with

its broad, unturned upper part, is typical of the early period.

Provenance: Purchased by John Franklin Goucher, Egypt, 1889

————————————————————————*J. V. C.*

39   GRINDING PALETTE
Egyptian (New Kingdom), 1570–1085 B.C.
Fine-grained black stone
Width: 5 ⅞ inches; Height: 1 ¼ inches
Lent by Goucher College, Baltimore

This rectangular stone object with a receding base is lightly depressed on top. It has the typical shape of palettes used to grind paint. (For a similar palette, see *Egypt's Golden Age: The Art of Living in the New Kingdom, 1558–1085 B.C.,* exh. cat., Museum of Fine Arts, Boston, 1982, 285, no. 393.)

Provenance: Purchased by Mrs. John Franklin Goucher, Egypt, 1889

————————————————————————*J. V. C.*

40   FIGURINE
Egyptian (Amarna Period), 1372–1355 B.C.
Reddish clay, baked
Height: 3 ½ inches; Greatest thickness: ⅛ inch
Lent by Goucher College, Baltimore (no. E.59.10)

42

43

44

41

The mold-made figure represents a man in a knee-length skirt, standing with his left arm bent across his body. The protruding chin, narrow chest, and bulging stomach are characteristic features of the art of the age of the heretic pharaoh, Akhenaton. The back of the piece is flat.

Provenance: Purchased by John Franklin Goucher, Egypt, 1889

————————————————————*J. V. C.*

41 MUMMY OF A YOUNG GIRL
Egyptian
Painted gesso, linen, partly gilt
Length: 43 inches
Lent by Goucher College, Baltimore (no. E1)

The upper part of the body is covered by a separate piece of cartonnage on which the face has been modeled and covered with gilt. (The head and torso are covered by a long wig and beads.) On the cartonnage of the mummy itself, below another series of beads, funerary scenes are painted in green, black, and red. This base was carefully wrapped with linen strips folded into bands one-half an inch wide and applied in a criss-cross pattern.

Provenance: Purchased by John Franklin Goucher, Egypt, 1889

————————————————————*J. V. C.*

42 SHROUD FRAGMENT
Egyptian
Black ink on linen
Length: 20 inches; Height: 2 ¾ inches
Lent by Goucher College, Baltimore (no. E.34)

Parts of the Book of the Dead were often inscribed on the bandages in which mummies were wrapped. Here, at left, two goddesses kneel beside a sun disc with downstreaming rays. In the next section, four gods are worshiped by a kneeling figure, in front of whom another god is seated on a structure. All of these figures are shown on a papyrus boat. At the right is an inscription.

Provenance: Purchased by John Franklin Goucher, Egypt, 1889

Selected Reference: Louise A. Kohn, "Goucher's Egyptian Collection," *Goucher Alumnae Quarterly* 11, 2 (February 1983):4.

————————————————————*J. V. C.*

45

43 YOKE
Pre-Columbian (Mexico, Veracruz style),
    A.D. 7th–9th century
Stone
Height: 4 ⅞ inches; Width: 15 inches; Length:
    16 ½ inches
Lent by Goucher College, Baltimore, Dr. John F.
    Goucher Collection

U-shaped yokes of stone, vertical palmas, and flat ax heads are thought to replicate details of the costume worn by athletes around their waists. The ceremonial ball game for which this yoke was used, known by the Aztecs as *tlachtli,* originated on the Gulf Coast and spread throughout Mexico.
    The yoke is carved with a human visage.

————————————————————*W. R. J.*

44 STANDING FIGURE
Pre-Columbian (Mexico, Aztec), A.D. 1350–1521
Basalt
Height: 17 ⅞ inches
Lent by Goucher College, Baltimore, Dr. John F.
    Goucher Collection

45 SEATED FIGURE
Pre-Columbian (South Mexico, Mixtec),
    A.D. 14th–15th century
Basalt
Height: 16 ¼ inches
Lent by Goucher College, Baltimore, Dr. John F.
    Goucher Collection

THOMAS FOOTER (1847–1923)
Cumberland

Thomas Footer's contributions to the commerce of his adopted city, Cumberland, have been discussed at length by local historians. Perhaps out of respect for his "unassuming" nature and his "strong aversion to notoriety," however, these writers have tended to neglect his accomplishments in private life.

Thomas Footer was born in Yorkshire, near Leeds, to an English paper manufacturer and his wife, James and Mary Footer. Orphaned at an early age, Thomas supported himself by working in textile mills and sought an education at night school, where he developed an abiding interest in chemistry and history, fields of relevance to his subsequent career. After his marriage to Elizabeth Booth and the birth of two sons, he immigrated with his family to America in 1870. He sought employment in mills in Philadelphia, Oswego Falls, and Harpers Ferry before settling in Cumberland, an auspicious choice of location, given the city's proximity to coal mines and its strategic situation at the hub of rail, canal, and road systems. There, Thomas Footer established a dyeing and dry-cleaning establishment, the Cumberland Dye Works, that grew from a one-room concern to a vast plant employing five hundred individuals and consuming 150 tons of coal every week. Branch depots were eventually opened in more than twenty cities to receive goods that were transported to the home plant for treatment.

Although local writers were unanimous in their praise of Thomas Footer's exemplary concern for the welfare of his employees and his commitment to various civic causes, only one author commented on his interests in art and literature. James Thomas, writing in 1923, observed that Footer had recently erected an addition to his house, in which he placed "one of the largest libraries and finest collections of books in Maryland, also a fine collection of antiques, ivories, rare paintings and pictures, rare books and publications and an unusual collection of ceramics and many other rare curios."

A further insight into Thomas Footer's character and interests is provided by the reminiscences of his granddaughter, Mrs. Cyril W. Keene. She recalls him as a warmhearted individual who loved beautiful works of art, which he purchased during the course of many travels, at times with the help of an agent, Mr. Evans. Despite his limited formal education, she remembers that in his later years he taught himself Latin and that he was an ardent bibliophile who specialized in collecting first editions. Her grandfather, admiring the Walterses' practice of opening their collections to the Baltimore public, had wished to provide a museum for Cumberland. The city government was unwilling to assume responsibility for the upkeep of the facility, however, and after Footer's death, the collections were dispersed—the library being given to Duke University and the art works sold privately. Today, Footer's residence and its wing still stand at 57 Decatur Street, bearing testimony to what might have been.

Suggestions for Further Reading: Matthew Page Andrews, *History of Maryland* (Chicago/Baltimore, 1925), 3:607; James W. Thomas and J. T. C. Williams, *History of Allegany County, Maryland* (Baltimore, 1923), 1:549–51.

—W.R.J.

JEAN-LÉON GÉRÔME
French, 1824–1904
46 *The Tulip Folly* (1882)
Oil on canvas
25 ¾ x 39 ⁵⁄₁₆ inches
The Walters Art Gallery 37.2612, Gift of
    Mrs. Cyril W. Keene

Gérôme, an academic realist painter, specialized in ancient and oriental genre compositions that were popularized through photogravures published by his dealer and father-in-law, Adolphe Goupil. In one of his rare ventures into the subject matter of the seventeenth century, Gérôme recreated a scene reminiscent of "tulipomania," the craze for tulips that reached its zenith in Holland from 1634 to 1637, when speculators bid as much as forty-six hundred *florins* for a single bulb. Here, a patrician officer protects an exceptional potted tulip, while soldiers trample a bed of tulips in the background. It has been suggested by P. ten-Doesschate Chu that this picture was inspired by Alexandre Dumas' novel, *La Tulipe Noire,* published in 1850.

Inscription: J. L. Gérôme

Provenance: Mary J. Morgan Sale, American Art Association, New York, 3–15 March 1886, lot 156 ($6,000); acquired for $1,650 by Mr. J. C. (or G.?) Evans on behalf of Mr. Thomas Footer, Cumberland; given to his daughter, Mrs. Cephas H. Glass, in 1923; by descent to her daughter, Mrs. Cyril W. Keene (1933)

Selected References: Manuscript catalogue, c.1883, 64 bis (as *Le Duel à la Tulipe*), Bibliothèque Nationale, Paris; Fanny Field Hering, *Gérôme* (New York, 1892), 242; Petra ten-Doesschate Chu, *French Realism and the Dutch Masters* (Utrecht, 1974), n. 37; Bernard Barryte, Jean-Léon Gérôme's *The Tulip Folly, The Walters Art Gallery Bulletin,* vol. 37, no. 3.

—B.B.

46

THE GARRETT FAMILY
Baltimore

The Garrett family is inextricably associated with the development of the economic, social, and cultural life of Baltimore. Robert Garrett (1783–1857), the patriarch of the family, was brought as a child from Ireland to this country and was raised by his mother on a farm in Cumberland County, Pennsylania. He arrived in Baltimore in 1801, to work as a clerk for a produce commission house. Within a couple of decades, he succeeded in founding Robert Garrett and Company, a firm that transported foods by Conestoga wagon to southwestern Pennsylvania, on the Cumberland trail. By 1840, Robert Garrett and Sons (as the firm came to be known) had diversified, with investments in railroads, particularly The Baltimore and Ohio Railroad, in international shipping and banking, in hotels, and even in shot towers.

John Work Garrett (1820–84), a son of Robert, joined the family business at age nineteen and in 1858 assumed control of the B&O. Although initially sympathetic to the South, he preserved his railroad's integrity during the Civil War, making it a vital force in the Union cause. J. W. Garrett was remarkably civic-minded, serving on the boards of The Maryland Institute, The Peabody Institute, and The Johns Hopkins University; he was also a founder of The Baltimore Y.M.C.A. His donations to The Peabody Institute included a series of plaster casts of ancient statuary, as well as bronze casts of Ghiberti's doors for the baptistery of Florence.

Garrett had several residences: one at Cathedral and Monument Streets in Mount Vernon Place; another, called "Montebello," was a country home on the Alameda and Thirty-third Street; and "Upper Montebello" was a farm farther north on Hillen Road, opposite Mount Pleasant Golf Course. The Mount Vernon Place residence was where he kept his art collection which, though large, was conventional for the time. It included works by Europeans, such as Andreas Achenbach, Gustave Brion, T. E. Duverger, and Florent Willems, as well as a few by Americans—Frederick Church, Thomas Cole, and John F. Kensett.

Of the third generation of Garretts, the most significant in the history of collecting were Robert Garrett (1847–96) and Thomas Harrison Garrett (1849–88). Robert, who succeeded his father as president of the B&O Railroad in 1884, was married to Mary Sloan Frick; they resided at 11 West Mount Vernon Place and at "Uplands," near Catonsville. Although the collection of Old Master paintings, now in The Baltimore Museum of Art, is generally associated with Mary Sloan Frick and her second husband, Dr. Henry Barton Jacobs, there were a number of important pictures hanging in the Mount Vernon Place house during Robert's life. Edmond Durand-Gréville recalled seeing, in 1887, portraits by Vigée-Lebrun, Nattier, and Drouais ("La Peinture aux Etats-Unis," *Gazette des Beaux Arts* 1⟨1887⟩:65–75).

T. Harrison was the operating manager of Robert Garrett and Sons, and the first Garrett to reside at "Evergreen," a late Classical-revival house on North Charles Street, bought by the family firm in 1878. While a college student, he began to form the now-celebrated Garrett coin collection. His interests also extended to rare books, oriental rugs, Japanese netsuke and inro, Chinese porcelain, autographs, and prints. So extensive were his holdings that he employed John W. M. Lee, once J. W. McCoy's private librarian, to serve him in the same capacity. T. Harrison Garrett died at the age of thirty-nine in a yachting accident, and the collections were passed on to his two sons, the second John Work Garrett (1872–1942) and the third Robert Garrett (1875–1961).

After their father's death, John Work, Robert, and a third brother, Horatio, who died in youth, were taken by their mother on an extended tour of Europe and the Near East; subsequently they attended Princeton University. Although John Work became a partner of Robert Garrett and Sons in 1896, his interests lay elsewhere. Three years later, he joined a Johns Hopkins University Medical School mission to the Philippines, which allowed him to pursue his lifelong study of ornithology, and between 1901 and 1933 he served the United States in a number of diplomatic posts in Europe and South America. While abroad, and following his retirement to "Evergreen," John Work avidly continued to enrich both the coin collection and the library; following the death of his mother in 1920, he and his wife, Alice Warder Garrett (1877–1952), transformed "Evergreen" into a veritable repository of the fine arts. In 1922/23, the local architect, Laurence Hall Fowler, and the Russian designer, Léon Bakst, were employed to convert "Evergreen's" gymnasium into a theater and its bowling alley into "The Far Eastern Room" for the display of Chinese porcelains and Japanese inro and netsuke. It was in the theater, with its vividly colored stenciled decoration by Bakst, that the resident "Musical Art Quartet" performed its concerts, beginning in 1928. Alice Garrett, in the meantime, pursued interests in contemporary painting, acquiring pictures by Pierre Bonnard, Jean Dufy, Léon Bakst, Ignacio Zuloaga, and A. Dunoyer de Segonzac, many of which she commissioned. An artist herself, she studied with Zuloaga and later enrolled at The Maryland Institute and at the Phillips Gallery in Washington, training under George Grosz, Reginald Marsh, and Jacques Maroger.

The third Robert, also a partner in the family firm, lived at "Attica," on Charles Street and Wyndhurst Road. He served the community as a trustee of both The Walters Art Gallery and The Baltimore Museum of Art, and was also the honorary president of the Society for the Preservation of Maryland Antiquities. Inheriting the Arabic and Persian manuscript collection, he devoted himself to interests in the fields of Middle Eastern archaeology and bibliophily. In 1899, Robert participated in an American archaeological expedition to Syria and later contributed funds that enabled The Baltimore Museum of Art to participate in the Antioch excavations. His loan of Arabic manuscripts to Princeton University in 1901 led to the establishment of the Department of Oriental Languages and Literature, and, in 1942, he donated to his alma mater his entire collection of rare books and manuscripts.

Suggestions for Further Reading: Harold A. Williams, *Robert Garrett and Sons* (Baltimore, 1965); *John Work Garrett and His Library at Evergreen* (Baltimore, 1944).

—*W. R. J.*

47 KORAN

Eastern Persian, 9th–10th century

Gold, tempera, ink on parchment

10 ¾ x 14 inches

Lent by The John Garrett Collection, Special Collections Division, The Milton S. Eisenhower Library, The Johns Hopkins University; on indefinite loan to the The Walters Art Gallery

Contained in this volume is the partial text of the Koran (*Qur'an*), the contents of which embody the fundamental precepts of the Muslim faith. According to tradition, divine inspiration induced the prophet Muhammad (d. A.D. 632) to formulate the moral and ethical injunctions serving as the spiritual code for adherents of the faith. This copy is a particularly splendid early example, opening with six elaborately embellished frontispiece pages written in gold *nashki* and *kufic*. The text continues in the latter script, completely in gold and framed with geometric or foliate interlace borders. Indicative of the high esteem with which this Koran was regarded is the inscription on the flap of the gilded and stamped binding, applied in the sixteenth century: "Let it not be touched except by those who are cleansed."

Recalling the circumstances of his acquisition of the codex, Robert Garrett wrote to Dorothy Miner, then the Keeper of Manuscripts at The Walters Art Gallery: "I remember clearly that the book was brought . . . to the Princeton Library and I happened just then to be working on my part of the report on the archaeological expedition . . . to Syria in 1899 to 1900 . . . it was not long before I made the purchase" (letter dated 7 July 1954). By 1938, Robert Garrett's collection of Arabic manuscripts had grown to some forty-five hundred items. Four years later, in order to take advantage of an opportunity to triple his holdings in this field, he sold the "Gold Koran" to his brother, John Work Garrett, thus managing both to enlarge his collection and to keep the magnificent codex in the family.

Provenance: Erased seals, inscriptions on fol.1; purchased by Robert Garrett in Princeton c.1905–06; sold to his brother, John Work Garrett, March 1942; bequeathed to The Johns Hopkins Library as part of the John Work Garrett Library; lent on indefinite deposit to The Walters Art Gallery, 1953.

Selected References: Philip K. Hitti, Nabih Amin Faris, Butrus 'Abd-al-Malik, *Descriptive Catalog of the Garrett Collection of Arabic Manuscripts* (Princeton, 1938), 359, no.1156; Phyllis Ackerman, *Exhibition of Persian Art*, The Iranian Institute (New York, 1944), 244; Kurt Weitzmann, "Islamische und koptische Einflüsse in einer Sinai-Handschrift des Johannes Klimakus," *Aus der Welt der Islamischen Kunst. Festschrift für Ernst Kühnel* (Berlin, 1959), 312–13, fig.15.

———————————— *L.M.C.R.*

47

JOHN CLIMACUS

48 *The Heavenly Ladder*

Greek, dated A.D. 1081

Tempera on parchment

10 ¾ x 7 ¾ inches

Lent by Princeton University Library (Garrett MS 16)

An early documented date and fine illustrations lend special interest to this copy of one of the most important Greek Christian treatises devoted to monastic spiritual ideals. The author, a monk whose surname derives from the title of his work (*klimax* signifying "ladder" in Greek), was abbot of Mount Sinai during the late sixth century. He is depicted twice in the Garrett manuscript, both times exhorting a group of monks to scale a ladder of metaphoric intent, based on the biblical reference to Jacob's ladder (Genesis 28:10ff.). As expounded and illustrated in the course of the objectives provided in the Greek text, the thirty rungs assigned to the ladder correspond to the number of years spent by Christ in private ministry; they also total the number of virtues to be adopted and vices to be conquered by aspirants to salvation. Toward the end of the manuscript, in a grand pictorial finale, monks are shown eagerly approaching the foot of the ladder, blissfully unaware of the impending fate awaiting some of their brethren, who are vividly depicted falling toward the jaws of a demonic dragon. Other monks steadfastly pursue their ascent toward ideal perfection, personified by Christ at the top of the ladder.

Provenance: Monastery of Kosinitza, latter nineteenth century; Joseph Baer, Frankfurt, c.1920; purchased from Baer by Robert Garrett; presented to the Princeton University Library, 1942

Selected References: John R. Martin, *The Illustrations of the Heavenly Ladder of John Climacus* (Princeton, 1954), *passim*; *Illuminated Greek Manuscripts from American Collections: An Exhibition in Honor of Kurt Weitzmann*, ed. Gary Vikan (Princeton, 1973), no.19.

———————————— *L.M.C.R.*

48

49 BIBLE

English, c.1260–70

Tempera, gold, and colored line drawings on parchment

9 ½ x 6 ¾ inches

Lent by Princeton University Library (Garrett MS 28)

The commingling of French influence with English traditions is well reflected in this manuscript, the distinguished Maryland ownership of which extended from Robert Gilmor, Jr. (d.1848), to Robert Garrett (d.1961). Of particular note is the inclusion of two psalm recensions, Gallican and Hebraic, which are placed side by side and endowed with two fine sets of figural and ornamental initials at the ten major divisions. Emphasis on the Gallican version is subtly indicated here by the use of exclusively historiated scenes rendered in tempera and gold. The colored line drawings in the Hebraic set of initials are also of note, however, for their imaginative calligraphic skill, which points the way to a major development in English book illustration of succeeding decades. In several instances, the choice of subject in the paired opening letters represents variations on a single theme. This is the case, for example, in the opening initials of Psalm 1, in which David as musician and David beheading Goliath appear beside an animated rendering of David aiming his sling at his giant foe.

Provenance: John and Arthur Arch, London booksellers, before 1830; bought by Obadiah Rich, Bostonian, American consul to Madrid and London bookseller for £4.14, 1832; bought by Robert Gilmor, Jr., for £5.5 in binding applied by O. Rich for 18 shillings,

49

50

51 BOOK OF HOURS

French, c.1425–30

Tempera and gold on parchment

8 ½ x 6 ¼ inches

Lent by Princeton University Library (Garrett MS 48)

The preference among French book patrons for expanded narrative subject matter, expressed increasingly from the fourteenth century on, is well exemplified in this Book of Hours for the use of Troyes. The contents are divided between the Arsenal Library in Paris (MS 647, 121 folios) and the Princeton University Library (Garrett MS 48, 105 folios). Influenced by the artistic genius of the Rohan Master, the pictorial program in the Garrett portion enriches prayers to the Virgin and to Christ, the Hours of the Passion, and the Vigils of the Dead. Each text section and major subdivision opens with a large miniature, bordered on all sides but the top by small panels containing figures related to the central theme. A highly unusual motif below the Betrayal adds particular interest to the opening page of the Hours of the Passion. Based on an incident cited in the Gospel of Saint Mark (14:51–52), it depicts a haloed figure identified by medieval writers as Saint John the Evangelist, shown abandoning his cloak as he hurries after Christ, whom all others have abandoned following Judas' vile act. Further references to the betrayal of Christ are implicit in the other two border scenes showing Saint Peter before the cock and with the servant-maid. Colorfully rendered in vivid detail, the emotional impact conveyed by these and subsequent participants in the Passion cycle parallels in its dramatic effect the im-

---

1832: William Gilmor; T. Harrison Garrett; Robert Garrett; presented to the Princeton University Library, 1942

Selected Reference: Adelaide Bennett, "The Place of Garrett 28 in Thirteenth-Century English Illumination" (Columbia University, diss.), 1973.

————————————————— *L.M.C.R.*

SENECA ET AL.

50 *Select Works*

English, late 12th–early 13th century

Tempera and gold on parchment

9 ¹⁄₁₆ x 6 ¼ inches

Lent by Princeton University Library

(Garrett MS 114)

This codex, which is in pristine condition, bears splendid witness to the twelfth-century revival of interest in Classical thought. Of note not only for its contents, but also for its fine script and historiated initials, the volume is still in its original calf-covered wooden binding; it also retains a contemporary double-thong bookmark. Early ownership by the Augustinian abbey of the Holy Cross at Waltham, Essex, is indicated by a pressmark and an inscription. An English origin, though not necessarily at Waltham, is suggested by the thick, white, velvet-surfaced parchment and the design of the small red-and-blue penwork initials. On the other hand, foreign influences of Byzantine, northeast French, and Belgian derivation permeate the style of the figures in the four vividly colored initials, all of which appear at the beginning of works by Seneca rather than of Cassiodorus or Solinus (who are also represented in this compilation of texts chosen for the treatment of questions pertaining to the effects of fate and chance on human destiny). The highly original choice of illustrative themes includes depictions of a cleric standing on the shoulders of a wild-haired youth, a wheel of fortune, the Roman emperor Claudius casting dice, and Nero ordering the death by bleeding of his former tutor, Seneca. In type and rendering, the dignified figures bear comparison with biblical and hagiographic counterparts in the initials of near-contemporary masterpieces from Winchester and St. Albans.

Provenance: Waltham abbey (Essex), 13th century; Sir Nicholas Bacon, c.1540; Sir John Holt of Redgrave, Suffolk, c.1680; inherited by George Holt Wilson of Redgrave Hall, Suffolk; his sale, London, 21 July 1910, no.156, to Quaritch; sold to Henry Yates Thompson, 31 July 1911; his sale, London, 1920, no.33, to L. C. Harper; J. Martini, Cat. 17 (1921), no.21, and Cat. 18 (1922), no.18; E. D. North; Robert Garrett; presented to the Princeton University Library, 1942

Selected References: *Illustrations from One Hundred Manuscripts in the Library of Henry Yates Thompson* (London, 1914), 4:9–10, pls.16–17; Seymour De Ricci and W. J. Wilson, *Census of Medieval and Renaissance Manuscripts in the United States and Canada* (New York, 1935), 1:887, no.114; N. R. Ker, *Medieval Libraries of Great Britain* (London, 1941), 107; Konrad Hoffmann, *The Year 1200*, exh. cat., The Metropolitan Museum of Art (New York, 1970), no.255; H. P. Kraus, *Cimelia*, Cat. 165 (New York, 1983), no.2, n.l.

————————————————— *L.M.C.R.*

Collection of the Garrett Family

omme labia mea
apies Et os meū
annūciabit laudē.

51

pression made on contemporary viewers by actual staged performances of this sequence of events in the life of Christ.

Provenance: John Boykett Jarman, his sale, London, 13 June 1864, no. 41, to Boone; Robert Garrett; presented to the Princeton University Library, 1942

Selected Reference: Dorothy Miner, *Illuminated Books of the Middle Ages and the Renaissance*, exh. cat., The Walters Art Gallery (Baltimore, 1949), no. 97.

———————————————— *L. M. C. R.*

GIOVANNI MARCANOVA
52 *Antiquitates*
North Italian (probably Padua), 1465
Pen and ink on parchment
14 ¼ x 10 ¼ inches
Lent by Princeton University Library (Garrett MS 158)

A Paduan physician, Giovanni Marcanova was responsible for this compilation of inscriptions found on Classical monuments in various parts of the Roman Empire. His work, which revives a tradition established in the ninth century, combines the results of his own findings with those of notable contemporary Italian humanists, such as the Verona antiquarian, Felice Feliciano. The latter, who was also keenly interested in the shaping of Roman letters, dedicated a special selection of inscriptions to Mantegna, whose interest in the subject is clearly apparent in the use of inscriptions on monuments depicted in his paintings. This rare copy of Marcanova's text, completed after an earlier unillustrated version of 1460, is based on the physician's autograph copy in

53

the Biblioteca Estense, Modena. Beautifully written in humanist minuscule, with titles in capitals based on those in Roman inscriptions, the compilation is in itself a highly revealing monument to the enthusiasm for Classical forms and lettering in Renaissance Italy.

Provenance: Collegio Romano, Rome, until 1870; W. M. Voynich; Robert Garrett, 1924; presented to the Princeton University Library, 1942

Selected Reference: De Ricci, *Census*, 1:897, no. 158; Dorothy E. Miner, Victor J. Carlson, P. W. Filby, *2,000 Years of Calligraphy*, exh. cat., The Walters Art Gallery (Baltimore, 1965), no. 44; H. van Mater Dennis, "The Garrett Manuscript of Marcanova," 113–126, and E. B. Lawrence, "The Illustrations of the Garrett and Modena Manuscripts of Marcanova," 127–31, in *Memoirs of the American Academy in Rome* 6 (1927).

———————————————— *L. M. C. R.*

53 BOOK OF HOURS
French, c. 1470
Tempera and gold on parchment
6 ⅞ x 4 ¾ inches
Lent by Princeton University Library (Garrett MS 55)

Like many lavishly illustrated books for personal devotion, this prayerbook was made for the use of a lady of high social status. Armorial devices in a number of miniatures and borders establish her identity as Marguerite of Angoulême (c. 1420–95), wife of John of Orléans, count of Angoulême, and grandmother of Francis I. The original owner is depicted toward the end of her

book in a striking, half-length reverent pose before the Savior. Her widow's garb indicates the completion of this portrait after the death of her husband in 1465. A highly personal sort of emphasis on death is found, further, in the depiction of a female, rather than the customary male corpse, in the representation of the Fight for the Soul before God's Throne of Judgment at the beginning of the Vigils of the Dead.

Stylistically, the fifteen fine miniatures in this prayerbook for Paris use reflect elements found in near-contemporary deluxe manuscripts from leading production centers, such as Bourges, Tours, and Poitiers. While the latest taste is reflected in the Italianate architectural settings and the choice of a night scene for the Betrayal, the particular function of this volume for use by a widow in mourning is underscored through a somber palette dominated by deep hues of blue, purple, and non-brilliant, painted gold.

Provenance: Marguerite of Angoulême; Charles Sauvageot through Pottier, his sale, Paris, 3 December 1860, no. 44; Ambroise Firmin-Didot, his sale, Paris, 1882, no. 16, to Labitte; Marcel Thévenin sale, Paris, 4 March 1903, no. 1; Robert Garrett; presented to the Princeton University Library, 1942

Selected References: Robert Garrett, "Recollections of a Collector," *Princeton University Chronicle* 10, 3 (April 1949):105; Dorothy Miner, *Illuminated Books of the Middle Ages and Renaissance*, exh. cat., The Walters Art Gallery (Baltimore, 1949), no. 116; John Plummer, with Gregory Clark, *The Last Flowering: French Painting in Manuscripts, 1420–1530*, exh. cat., The Pierpont Morgan Library (New York, 1982), no. 65.

———————————————— *L. M. C. R.*

52

54 *TESTAMENT OF AMYRA, SULTAN OF NICH HEMEDY* and *THE DEBATE BETWEEN SULTANS YLDRAM PAYAZIT AND GREMY*

Flemish work in England, c.1482
Parchment, covered by contemporary binding of
brown calf over boards
10 x 6 ⅝ inches
Lent by Princeton University Library (Garrett MS 168)

Robert Garrett's interests in history and the Near East are reflected in a highly original manner in this slim volume containing an account of the death of Muhammad II and the ensuing political consequences. Documented within the text as having been composed in Constantinople on 12 September 1481, the two-part dispatch is here preserved in an early French translation from the Italian. The single illumination, a floral border on gold ground at the beginning of the second portion of the text, is of particular interest for the inclusion of the arms of Edward V as prince of Wales. Since Edward was one of the unfortunate murder victims of the aspiring Richard, duke of Gloucester, a date prior to the homicide in the Tower of London in August or September 1483, is established for the manuscript. Its binding, blind-stamped with fleurs-de-lis and dragons encased in triangles, has been attributed on the basis of similar examples to a Fleming, John Guilbert (called Meese), who is known to have worked with William Caxton shortly after the return of the noted printer to England in the late 1470s, after an extended residence in Bruges.

Provenance: Presentation copy for Edward V, then prince of Wales: ownership entries by his sisters, Elizabeth of York (1465–1503) and Cecily (1469–1507): Sir Henry Ingilby, Bart., at Ripley Castle, Yorkshire, latter 19th century: his sale, London, 21 October 1920, no.5, to Quaritch: bought by Robert Garrett, 1936: presented to the Princeton University Library, 1942

Selected References: De Ricci, *Census*, 2:2295, no.168: Dorothy E. Miner, *The History of Bookbinding. 525–1950 A.D.*, exh. cat., The Walters Art Gallery (Baltimore 1957), no.175: Bond and Faye, *Supplement*, 313, no.168.

——————————————— L.M.C.R.

55 *JÓNSBÓK*

Icelandic, 15th century
Tempera, gold, silver on parchment
5 ½ x 4 ⅜ inches
Lent by Princeton University Library (Garrett MS P-62)

The Icelandic code of law known as the *Jónsbók* is named after one of its presumed chief authors, Jón Einarsson, emissary of the Norwegian king, Magnus VII. Ratified after considerable debate in A.D. 1281, the code remained in effect virtually unchanged for more than four hundred years. Its eleven sections regulate all areas of human concern, ranging from parliamentary procedure and godliness to taxation, inheritance and land rights, ownership of driftwood and beached whales, commerce, homicide, and theft. Traditionally, each of these legislative categories in texts that have come down to us opened with an ornamental initial. Since the *Jónsbók* is preserved in many copies, it constitutes the largest single group of illustrated medieval codices of Icelandic origin.

The fifteenth-century exemplar acquired by Robert Garrett is a fine representative of this tradition. It contains handsome initials of both abstract and figural design in combinations of vivid colors with gold and silver. Of special interest among the latter are depictions of a legislator and of a thief hanging on a gallows. Colorful line-fillers further enhance the appearance of this portable copy of the law code, the first printed edition of which was issued in 1578. The excellent condition of the sixteenth-century, blind-stamped, brown calf binding on this manuscript attests to the respect accorded the volume by successive owners,

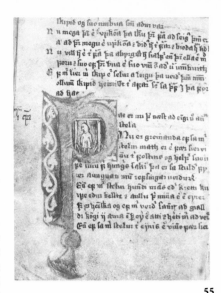

55

some of whom recorded their names on a preliminary flyleaf.

Provenance: Flyleaf ownership notes by Olafor Thorlahfson, Magnus Thorleiffsson and others: Sir Thomas Maryon Wilson, Bart., 17th century, bookplate: acquired by Robert Garrett in 1931: presented to the Princeton University Library, 1942

Selected References: Bond and Faye, *Supplement*, 309, no.62: cf. *Icelandic Sagas. Eddas. and Art*, exh. cat., The Pierpont Morgan Library (New York and Reykjavik, 1982), 41–44.

——————————————— L.M.C.R.

IGNACIO ZULOAGA
Spanish, 1870–1945

56 *Study for the Decoration for the first act of "Goyescas"* (1917)

Oil on canvas
46 x 48 ¾ inches
Lent by The Evergreen House Foundation, Baltimore

Zuloaga taught himself to paint by copying pictures in the Prado and the Louvre. Influenced by El Greco, Velázquez, and particularly Goya, he specialized in Spanish genre scenes and landscapes, achieving fame during the final years of the nineteenth century. Zuloaga's broad and painterly style and the emotional realism of his landscapes reflect his belief "that the painter is entitled to arrange, compose, magnify, and exalt those elements that go to make up a given scene." Zuloaga's capacity for dramatic characterization attracted an international clientele, and he became one of the most fashionable portrait painters of his day.

The artist's first attempt at theatrical decoration, this landscape was suggested by the 1916 opera, *Goyescas: Los Majos Enamorados,* by Zuloaga's countryman, Enrique Granados (1867–1916). Zuloaga incor-

54

porated motifs from several of Goya's tapestry designs, including *The Swing, The Parasol, The Straw Manikin,* and *La Pradera de San Isidro,* which had also served as the initial inspiration for the piano suite upon which Granados had developed his opera (see J. R. Longland, "Granados and the Opera *Goyescas,*" *Hispanic Notes* 5, ⟨1945⟩:95–112).

Provenance: Alice Garrett

Selected Reference: Enrique Lafuente Ferrari, *La vida y el arte de Ignacio Zuloaga* (Madrid, 1950), 72, 191, 236 (no. 437).

—————————————————————*B.B.*

56

57

THE GARRETTS' ORIENTAL COLLECTION

The Johns Hopkins University collection of oriental art at Evergreen House was formed by T. Harrison Garrett (1849–88) and his son, John Work Garrett (1872–1942). Formerly on display in the main house, the collection was removed to the Far East Room in 1923, where it has since remained on permanent display.

Although the elder Garrett's original records of purchase were probably lost during the Baltimore Fire (1904), a handwritten catalogue of his collection does exist. Probably compiled by Edward Greey (a mid-nineteenth-century importer of oriental art and author of popular books on Japan), the comprehensive and scholarly descriptions reveal that numerous works of art were purchased as "modern." Further, we find that the direct source for many inro was the greatest master of the lacquerer's art, Shibata Zeshin (1807–91).

While visiting Japan and the Philippines on behalf of a Johns Hopkins Hospital Commission in 1899, John Work Garrett purchased additional objects. In Japan, he met Masayuki Kataoka, who had formerly catalogued books and "rolls" for the South Kensington Museum (now the Victoria and Albert Museum), London. Together, the collector and historian visited a lacquerer, and subsequently John Work Garrett began to augment his father's collection. Following his return to the United States, the younger Garrett continued to employ Kataoka as his agent, and it was through this arrangement that the formidable collection of mask netsuke was formed. The collection was further enhanced by the original watercolors supplied by Kataoka for all of John Work Garrett's purchases.

Although the collection is representative of all oriental countries, both T. Harrison and John Work Garrett appear to have been most keenly attracted to the so-called "minor" arts of Japan, and it is this segment of the collection that is of primary significance. In addition to its importance in size and scope, the Garrett is one of the few "first generation" collections in the United States to have remained intact. Although it was formed by two generations of collectors, the collection represents a consistency of taste and virtually identical methods of acquisition that are interesting to note.

—————————————————————————————————————*S.G.T.*

57 PORCELAIN JAR

Chinese (Kangxi Period), 1662–1722

Height: 9 ½ inches

Lent by The Johns Hopkins University,
The Evergreen House (H.G. 28)

This underglaze blue-and-white porcelain jar of rounded form and cover is molded with hexagonal medallions and painted with female figures, boys, and potted flowers. An artemisia leaf mark is on the base.

Provenance: T. Harrison Garrett; John Work Garrett

———————————————*S.G.T.*

58 INRO

Japanese, 17th century

Height: 2 ½ inches; Width: 2 ⅛ inches

Lent by The Johns Hopkins University, The Evergreen House (K 4B)

This small, four-case inro is decorated on the rubbed *nashiji* ground (a sprinkled ground of powdered gold covered with a reddish-yellow lacquer) with stylized *kiku* (chrysanthemum) blooms. The *kiku* blossoms are in black *takamakie* (a raised, sprinkled design) and exhibit traces of original gilding.

NETSUKE

Japanese, early 19th century

Height: 1 x 1 ½ inches

The ivory netsuke depicts *Gama Senin* (a Taoist Immortal endowed with magical powers), seated, holding his attribute, a toad.

OJIME

An ivory bead simulating coral

Provenance: John Work Garrett

Selected Reference: Forthcoming publication by Susan G. Tripp and Neil Davey on the Garrett Japanese art collection.

———————————————*S.G.T.*

59 INRO

Japanese, 18th century

Height: 3 inches; Width: 2 ⅝ inches

Lent by The Johns Hopkins University,
The Evergreen House (G 8)

A four-case inro with a *kinji* (bright gold) ground is decorated with two rats in brown and silver *togidashi* (a sprinkled design overlaid with thick lacquer and heavily polished to bring the surfaces flush). Familiar in Japanese myths and legends, the rat is often associated with *Daikoku* (the god of wealth), or as the first sign of the zodiac.

Signed: (on the side): *Shiomi Masabige:* (and, in seal form): *Shiomi Masanari*

NETSUKE

Japanese, 18th century

Height: 1 ⅜ inches; Width: 2 inches

The ivory netsuke depicts a rat and two straw hats on a winnowing basket.

OJIME

Cloisonné bead

Provenance: T. Harrison Garrett; John Work Garrett

Selected Reference: Forthcoming publication by Susan G. Tripp and Neil Davey on the Garrett Japanese art collection.

———————————————*S.G.T.*

60 MASK NETSUKE

Japanese, 18th century

Height: 1 ¾ inches; Width: 1 ¼ inches

Lent by The Johns Hopkins University,
The Evergreen House (KM 71)

Carved in wood, the *Namanari* mask portrays a female demon from the *Nō* theater. The short horns rising from either side of the head, the jutting jaw, reddened mouth, four fangs of lacquered gold, and the wildly penetrating but humanly rendered eyes inlaid with brass are the characteristics of this enraged and jealous woman. To increase the half-woman/half-demon effect, the face is painted vermilion and the hair is slightly disheveled.

As with any netsuke, the utilitarian nature of the toggle required artistic license in the portrayal of the character. The horns are slightly adapted to the use of the netsuke, as with other horned female demons.

Signed: *Deme Uman, tenka ichi* (first under heaven)

Provenance: John Work Garrett

Selected Reference: Forthcoming publication by Susan G. Tripp and Neil Davey on the Garrett Japanese art collection.

———————————————*S.G.T.*

58   **59**

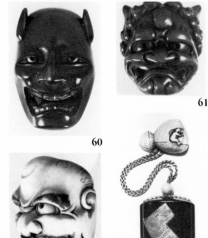

60

61

62

63

61 MASK NETSUKE

Japanese, late 18th–early 19th century

Height: 3 ⅜ inches; Width: 3 inches

Lent by The Johns Hopkins University, The Evergreen House (KM 172)

This carved-wood netsuke depicts an *oni* (an impish creature or demon). Features of the *oni* are a square head, two horns, sharp teeth, and a hairy body. The *oni* is found in many Japanese legends and is often shown being chased from a house at the New Year by the throwing of peas, representing the casting out of ill luck. The character also appears in several *Nō* plays.

Provenance: John Work Garrett

Selected Reference: Forthcoming publication by Susan G. Tripp and Neil Davey on the Garrett Japanese art collection.

———————————————*S.G.T.*

62 MASK NETSUKE

Japanese, late 18th–early 19th century

Height: 1 ⅝ inches; Width: 1 ¼ inches

Lent by The Johns Hopkins University,
The Evergreen House (KM 51)

This netsuke, carved in ivory, represents a *Shishiguchi* mask, derived from the legendary Chinese lion-like animal that is often shown in conjunction with peony plants. The *shishi* are guardians of sacred places.

Used only in the *Nō* play, *Skakkyo,* an actor wears the *Shishiguchi* mask and dances on the stage among red and white peony plants. The actor wears a red wig with the mask, as seen on an inro (no.67).

Provenance: John Work Garrett

Selected Reference: Forthcoming publication by Susan G. Tripp and Neil Davey on the Garrett Japanese art collection.

—————————————————————————— *S. G. T.*

63 INRO

Japanese, probably 19th century
Height: 3 ⅛ inches; Width: 2 ¼ inches
Lent by The Johns Hopkins University,
    The Evergreen House (K 16A)

A four-case inro with a *rōiro* (a lustrous black lacquer) ground is decorated with a folded kimono and, on the reverse, with a storage box and an open fan. The kimono is elaborately decorated with flowers and waves in gold, silver, and red *takamakie* (a raised, sprinkled design); the box is decorated in brown *takamakie,* gold *hiramakie* (a very slightly raised, sprinkled design), and *karakusa* (arabesques). The fan is in brown *takamakie* and *aogai* (an inlaid, iridescent, blue-green shell). The interior is of red lacquer.

64

Signed: (in *chinkinbori,* a black lacquer engraved and then filled with gold): *Koma Kyuhaku saku*

NETSUKE

Japanese, early 19th century
Height: 1 ⅜ inches; Width: 2 ⅛ inches

An ivory netsuke shows a monkey emerging from a chestnut, with a smaller chestnut to the side.

OJIME

Coral bead

Provenance: John Work Garrett

Selected Reference: Forthcoming publication by Susan G. Tripp and Neil Davey on the Garrett Japanese art collection.

—————————————————————————— *S. G. T.*

64 INRO

Japanese, probably 19th century
Height: 3 ½ inches; Width: 2 ½ inches
Lent by The Johns Hopkins University,
    The Evergreen House (G 45)

This four-case inro, with a rich ground of reddish-yellow lacquer over irregularly shaped flakes of gold, is decorated with a plum branch with blossoms and a knot. The knot and branch continue around the inro and are embellished with gold and colored *takamakie* (a raised, sprinkled design) and with inlaid coral and *raden* (mother-of-pearl).

Signed: *Kanshosai*

NETSUKE

Japanese, 19th century
Diameter: 1 ⅞ inches

A two-part *manjū* (a netsuke in the shape of a rice cake) is carved in *shishiaibori* (undercutting), with a *karako* (Chinese boy) holding a pup; the reverse shows two seated pups.

Signed: *Hogyoku saku*

OJIME

A mask of the female demon *Hannya* is carved from narwhal ivory.

Provenance: T. Harrison Garrett; John Work Garrett

Selected Reference: Forthcoming publication by Susan G. Tripp and Neil Davey on the Garrett Japanese art collection.

—————————————————————————— *S. G. T.*

65

65 MASK NETSUKE

Japanese, 19th century
Height: 2 ¼ inches; Width: 1 ¾ inches
Lent by The Johns Hopkins University,
    The Evergreen House (KM 128)

The red-lacquer mask of *Hyottoko* well defines this comic character from Japanese legends and plays. *Hyottoko* masks are used in *Kyogen* plays, comic interludes between the *Nō* dramas.

Signed: *Sosai*

Provenance: John Work Garrett

Selected Reference: Forthcoming publication by Susan G. Tripp and Neil Davey on the Garrett Japanese art collection.

—————————————————————————— *S. G. T.*

66 INRO

Japanese, 19th century
Height: 3 ½ inches; Width: 2 ¼ inches
Lent by The Johns Hopkins University,
    The Evergreen House (G 3)

This four-case inro has a very unusual ground of ultramarine blue sprinkled with *hirame* (irregular flakes of gold). The iris and butterfly design is delicately treated in gold and colored *hiramakie* (a very slightly raised, sprinkled design) and *e-nashiji* (*nashiji* or gold powder in the design, not in the ground). The interior is of *nashiji* (a sprinkled ground of powdered gold covered with a reddish-yellow lacquer).

Signed: *Taira Shusai*

NETSUKE
Japanese, 19th century
Height: 1 ¼ inches; Width: 1 inches

The wood netsuke is in the form of a seated badger.

Signed: *Masakazu* (*Gifu* school)

OJIME
An elongated, stamped-metal bead

Provenance: T. Harrison Garrett; John Work Garrett

Selected Reference: Forthcoming publication by Susan G. Tripp and Neil Davey on the Garrett Japanese art collection.

———————————————— *S. G. T.*

67 INRO
Japanese, 19th century
Height: 3 ½ inches; Width: 2 ⅛ inches
Lent by The Johns Hopkins University,
    The Evergreen House (G 33)

A four-case inro is decorated on the *kinji* (polished gold) ground with a *Nō* dancer wearing a *Shishiguchi* mask and performing a scene from the play, *Shakkyo.* The *shishi,* a lion-like creature, is shown frolicking among peonies before a kneeling noble-man. The design is of gold and slightly col-ored *takamakie* (a raised, sprinkled design), with the mask of gold metalwork. The interior is of *nashiji* (a sprinkled ground of powdered gold covered with a reddish-yellow lacquer).

Signed: *Kakosai*

NETSUKE
Japanese, 19th century
Height: 1 ¾ inches; Width: ⅞ inches

Carved from a stag-antler, the netsuke por-trays the standing figure of *Okame* (god-dess of mirth).

OJIME
A glazed ceramic bead

Provenance: T. Harrison Garrett; John Work Garrett

Selected Reference: Forthcoming publication by Susan G. Tripp and Neil Davey on the Garrett Japanese art collection.

———————————————— *S. G. T.*

68 INRO
Japanese, 1807–91
Height: 2 ½ inches; Width: 2 ½ inches
Lent by The Johns Hopkins University, The Evergreen
    House (G 32)

The two-case inro with a *rōiro* ground (a lustrous black lacquer) is decorated with a *Nō* mask, and on the reverse shows mask carver's tools. The tools are of gold and slightly colored *takamakie* (a raised, sprin-kled design) and *sabejinuri* (lacquer simu-lating metal). The interior is of *kinji* (a polished gold ground).

Signed: (in scratched characters): *Zeshin*

NETSUKE
Japanese, 19th century
Diameter: 1 ¾ inches

A two-part ivory *manjū* (a netsuke in the shape of a rice cake) is carved in *shishiai-bori* (undercutting), with *Okame* (goddess of mirth) seated and holding a fan. The re-verse is carved with *kadomatsu* (New Year decorations of pine and bamboo).

Inscribed: *Hoshin*

66

67

68

OJIME
Stamped-metal bead.

Provenance: T. Harrison Garrett; John Work Garrett

Selected Reference: Forthcoming publication by Susan G. Tripp and Neil Davey on the Garrett Japanese art collection.

———————————————— *S. G. T.*

MARY FRICK JACOBS (1851–1936)
Baltimore

While visiting the United States in 1887, the French art critic, Edmond Durand-Gréville, made two stops in Baltimore's Mount Vernon Place: one at the residence of Robert Garrett, and the other at the gallery of William T. Walters. At the former, he was drawn to portraits by the French eighteenth-century artists, Madame Vigée-Lebrun, Nattier and Drouais.

It is not known whether Robert Garrett, then president of the B&O Railroad, or Mary Frick, his wife since 1872, was responsible for initiating the family art collection. Certainly its development must be credited to the latter. Robert Garrett died in 1896 and, six years later, the widow remarried. Her second husband, Dr. Henry Barton Jacobs, was a specialist in thoracic medicine, who had come to Baltimore to attend Robert Garrett as his private physician and had remained to teach at The Johns Hopkins Hospital.

Committed to her role as doyenne of Baltimore society in the early twentieth century, Mary Frick Jacobs allotted her time among her various residences: the Mount Vernon Place house; "Uplands," a country house near Catonsville; "Whiteholme," a villa in Newport, Rhode Island, built by John Russell Pope in 1904; and an apartment in Paris. To provide facilities necessary for receiving visitors (a ballroom, a theater, a library, and a grand drawing room), 11 West Mount Vernon Place, which had already been expanded by Stanford White at the time of her first marriage, underwent in 1902 yet another addition, this time by Pope. Quantities of eighteenth-century-style furniture, both period and revival, were purchased, together with Dresden porcelains, silver services, and ormolu fixtures.

Correspondence preserved in the archives of The Baltimore Museum of Art confirms that the collection of paintings underwent its principal growth between 1900 and 1916. The two major sources were T. J. Blakeslee (of Blakeslee Galleries, 665 Fifth Avenue, New York) and Eugene Fischof (of 30 rue St. Lazare, Paris, and of the Hotel Cambridge, New York). Blakeslee obtained most of the English portraits for Mrs. Jacobs, while Fischof served as an agent in Europe, acquiring paintings from various sources, including the Galerie Sedelmeyer in 1916.

America's entry into World War I brought to a close both the social life over which Mrs. Jacobs had presided and the conventions that she had so zealously sought to maintain. Her later years were spent in service to the Episcopal church and to the community. She was especially interested in children's causes, among them the Robert Garrett Hospital for Children and the Eudowood Sanitorium in Baltimore, and her annual Christmas parties for the city's newsboys became part of Baltimore's folklore.

Both Mrs. Jacobs and her husband were interested in The Baltimore Museum of Art; she was a founding member and he was eventually president of its board of trustees. Shortly before her death, Mrs. Jacobs offered to the museum the principal works in her collection: Rembrandt's portrait of his son, Titus; the remarkable painting by Frans Hals, and several other Dutch and Flemish works; the English portraits by Raeburn, Romney, and Hoppner; several Italian works, including two unusual Guardis, the Canaletto, and a Botticelli studio-piece; and the extraordinary selection of French eighteenth-century masterpieces by Quentin de la Tour, Hubert Robert, Fragonard, Greuze, Nattier, and many others.

The remainder of her collection and the household furnishings were sold at auction in 1940, after her husband's death.

Suggestions for Further Reading: E. Durand-Gréville, "La peinture aux Etats-Unis," *Gazette des Beaux-Arts* (1887), 2:251; Margie H. Luckett, *Maryland Women* (Baltimore, 1931), 215–18; "Estates of the Late Dr. and Mrs. Henry Barton Jacobs, 7, 9, 11 and 13 W. Mt. Vernon Place," Sale, Sam W. Pattison & Co. (Baltimore, 10–12 December, 1940); John Dorsey, *Mount Vernon Place* (Baltimore, 1983), 12–23.

—— *W. R. J.*

69

JACQUES-ANDRÉ-JOSEPH-CAMELOT AVED
French, 1702–77
69 *Monsieur d'Aguesseau de Fresnes*
Oil on canvas
51 x 39 inches
Lent by The Baltimore Museum of Art, Mary Frick
    Jacobs Collection

Formerly ascribed to Louis-Michel van Loo (1707–71), this painting has now been attributed to Aved by Gertrude Rosenthal. Aved was born in Douai and trained in Amsterdam and Paris; he devoted his career to portraiture. Among his patrons were Louis XV and Holland's Stadhouder, William IV,

although more frequently the patrons were members of the nobility, as was the case for this work. Henri-Francois d'Aguesseau (1668–1751) was a notable member of the *Parlement,* serving as its advocate general in 1690. Alternately in favor and disgrace, he served as chancellor of France three times during his long public career. In visual allusion to the contributions to French jurisprudence for which he was famous, d'Aguesseau is shown holding a book—possibly his legal textbook, *Instruction à mes enfants.* The sense of spontaneity generated by the sitter's direct and attentive gaze is enhanced by Aved's characteristic facility in depicting rich fabrics and typical still-life elements in his portraits.

This portrait was acquired through Eugene Fischof to adorn the mantel of the library of the Jacobs residence at Mount Vernon Place.

Provenance: Purchased by Mrs. Jacobs from Eugene Fischof, Paris (dealer), 1910

Selected References: Henry Barton Jacobs, *The Collection of Mary Frick Jacobs* (Baltimore, 1938), no.16; Letter from Gertrude Rosenthal (The Baltimore Museum of Art).

—————————————————————————— *B.B.*

ABRAM EISENBERG   (1860–1933)

Baltimore

One of the first Baltimore collectors to pursue Impressionist paintings was Abram Eisenberg. Born in Chibbish, Hungary, Eisenberg was brought to the United States as a child and was raised in Lonaconing, near Cumberland. He moved to Baltimore as a young man, eventually establishing the retail business, "Eisenberg's Underselling Store," at 213–19 West Lexington Street, which he operated for thirty-five years. In about 1902, he lived at Mrs. Rose Etting's boarding house (1627 Madison Avenue), which at that time was also the residence of the future collector, Jacob Epstein. Following his marriage to Helen Gutman, Eisenberg moved to 2405 Linden Avenue, where he raised his family and displayed his first art acquisitions. Eventually he settled at 6317 Park Heights Avenue.

Though the fashionable Barbizon and The Hague schools of painting initially drew his attention, Eisenberg eventually turned to the Impressionists. He bought two major Monets (*Charing Cross Bridge* and *Waterloo Bridge*), a Renoir, a Mary Cassatt, and a Childe Hassam.

Following her husband's death in 1933, Mrs. Eisenberg continued to enrich the collection with such works as Corot's *The Wreath of Flowers* and with several English portraits. In 1967, she presented the collection to The Baltimore Museum of Art, in memory of her husband.

Suggestion for Further Reading: *The New York Times* (27 January 1933).

—————————————————————————— *W.R.J.*

PIERRE AUGUSTE RENOIR
French, 1841–1919
70   *Child with a Hoop*   (c.1875)
Oil on canvas
24 ¼ x 19 ¼ inches
Lent by The Baltimore Museum of Art, The Helen
        and Abram Eisenberg Collection

In 1862, Renoir enrolled in the Ecole des Beaux Arts and entered the studio of Charles Gleyre. There he met the future inventors of Impressionism, Claude Monet, Sisley, and Bazille, with whom Renoir's career is closely associated and with whom he shared many theoretical concerns regarding spontaneity and color.

The Eisenberg painting is characteristic of Renoir's many entrancing portraits of children. The luminous quality of the youthful flesh is built up as a complex fabric of varicolored strokes, which the artist described as being knitted together (*tricotés*). The fragility of this evanescent bloom contrasts with the rich background tonality. The emphasis on the delicate beauty of the child accords with Renoir's idea that "a picture ought to be a loveable thing, joyous and pretty . . . There are enough boring things in the world without our fabricating still more."

Signed: (lower right): *Renoir*

Provenance: Mr. and Mrs. Abram Eisenberg

Selected References: François Daulte, *Auguste Renoir Catalogue Raisonné*, 5 vols. (Lausanne, 1971), 1, no.122; Wildenstein Gallery, *Renoir, The Gentle Rebel* (New York, 1974), no.15.

70

—————————————————————————— *B.B.*

JACOB EPSTEIN   (1864–1945)

Baltimore

One of Baltimore's most dramatic success stories concerns Jacob Epstein, who arrived in the United States almost penniless and, eventually amassing a fortune, became one of Baltimore's most generous benefactors.

Epstein's father was a drayman who hauled grain from Tauroggen, Lithuania, to Königsberg and Tilsit, Germany. To avoid military service, Jacob fled from his native Tauroggen in 1879 and came to this country with a friend, Isaac Charles Klein. Initially, he supported himself as a peddler, selling household goods in Western Maryland, Pennsylvania, and West Virginia, but eventually he established a shop at 48 West Barre Street. As a result of his remarkable business acumen and his reputation for integrity, the enterprise prospered, becoming the "Baltimore Bargain House" in 1881 and the "American Wholesale Corporation" in 1919. Ten years later, he was able to retire from business.

Jacob Epstein's involvement in the community was varied: he served on the Board of Supervisors of City Charities in 1906 and, three years later, he personally guaranteed $10,000 to induce the Metropolitan Opera Company to perform in Baltimore. Epstein contributed to many charities, and was particularly interested in those pertaining to Jews and—perhaps because of his high regard for Cardinal Gibbons—to Roman Catholics.

Epstein married Lena Weinberg in 1888 and bought a house on West Fayette Street. As he prospered, he moved, acquiring in 1908 an impressive house at 2532 Eutaw Place. It was here that he hung his art collection, allocating the Old Masters to the "Moorish Room," with its dark red color scheme, and the French paintings to the white-and-gold drawing room. His initial purchases in nineteenth-century paintings included De Neuville's *Officers Reconnoitering,* a version of *The Last Hours of a Condemned Man* by the popular Hungarian, Mihaly Munkacsy, and a *Charge of Arabs* by Adolph Schreyer. At the opening exhibition of The Baltimore Museum of Art in 1923, he lent a *Bergers d'Arcadie* by J. B. C. Corot, *Arc-en-Ciel* by J. C. Cazin, and a *Reverie* by The Hague School painter, Josef Israels. It was in the later twenties that Epstein acquired the Old Master pictures. In 1927 he obtained Van Dyck's *Rinaldo and Armida,* formerly in the collection of Charles I, from Knoedler and Company, and, in the same year, he purchased Raphael's portrait, *Emilia Pia de Montefeltro,* from F. Kleinberger and Company, New York. Other works to enter the collection at this time were the Sustermans *Portrait of a Nobleman of the Medici Family,* Titian's *Portrait of a Gentleman,* and works by Hals, Tintoretto, Veronese, and Reynolds, many of which were purchased from Joseph Duveen. Epstein's acquisitions in the field of sculpture included several Rodins, among them *The Thinker,* a number of large-scale pieces by the animalier A. L. Barye, and a collection of miniature works by Louis Rosenthal who, like Jacob Epstein, was from Lithuania.

Epstein's involvement with The Baltimore Museum of Art was of long standing. Appointed to the commission to erect a new museum building in 1924, he unsuccessfully lobbied for a site in Druid Hill Park rather than the Wyman Park location preferred by Dr. Henry Barton Jacobs and his associates. Nevertheless, most of his major pictures were placed on long-term loan in the new museum and were subsequently bequeathed to the institution.

Suggestions for Further Reading: Lester S. Levy, *Jacob Epstein* (Baltimore, 1978); *The Jacob Epstein Collection,* published by Jacob Epstein (Baltimore, 1939).

—*W. R. J.*

FRANS HALS

Dutch, 1581/85–1666

71 *Portrait of a Woman* (1634)

Oil on canvas

43 x 32 ½ inches

Lent by The Baltimore Museum of Art, Jacob Epstein
Collection

A student of the artist and writer Karel van Mander, Hals enjoyed contemporary renown, which faded rapidly after his death but was revived during the nineteenth century, when the artist was recognized as one of the leading masters of the Dutch Golden Age. Hals is best known for the vivid portraits that comprise the majority of his surviving oeuvre.

Dating from the 1630s, when Hals was at the height of his popularity, this work displays the bravura of brushwork and incisive delineation of character that are the artist's hallmarks. The exuberance demon-strated in his earlier portraits became more restrained during this phase of his development. Simplifying his forms and using an increasingly monochromatic palette, he created images of modest grandeur.

Slive suggests that the cropped *Portrait of a Man* in the Budapest Museum of Fine Arts is the pendant of the Epstein portrait.

Inscription: *AETA SVAE 28/AN⁰ 1634*

Provenance: Count André Mniszech, Paris; F. Kleinberger (dealer), Paris; A. de Ridder, Cronberg, near Frankfurt-am-Main; sale, de Ridder, Paris (Petit), 2 June 1924, no.23; Joseph Duveen, New York; from whom acquired by Jacob Epstein, 1924

Selected References: Wilhelm von Bode, *Studien zur Geschichte der holländischen Malerei* (Brunswick, 1883), 83, no.59; C. Hofstede de Groot, *Catalogue Raisonné* (London, 1910), 3:109, no.375; W. R. Valentiner, *Frans Hals Paintings in America* (Westport, 1936), no.45; Seymour Slive, *Frans Hals,* 3 vols. (London, 1974), vol.3, no.96, pl.157.

71

———————————————————————— *B.B.*

JAMES TEACKLE DENNIS   (1865–1918)

Baltimore

James Teackle Dennis was born into a prominent Maryland family and was educated at Lafayette College in Easton, Pennsylvania. In 1893, he married Ida Lee Wade, who is featured as one of the belles of Baltimore in the murals in Shriver Hall on The Johns Hopkins University campus. Following family tradition, Dennis studied for the bar and served briefly as state's attorney for Somerset County. He was primarily interested in Egyptology, however, which he studied at Hopkins from 1896 to 1903. Travel to Egypt in 1903 stimulated his enthusiasm for archaeological fieldwork and led him to offer his assistance to the Egypt Exploration Society, which was commencing excavation at the Eleventh Dynasty burial complex of Mentuhotep, at Deir el-Bahari. From 1905 to 1907, Dennis served as assistant to field director Edouard Naville, cataloguing wall fragments and photographing *ostraca* and inscriptions. On several occasions, he was appointed field director in full charge of the expedition. Dennis wrote many letters to his family, describing the social delights of Luxor, then a fashionable winter resort, and relating the excitement of the exploration, such as the discovery in 1907 of the Hathor shrine, with paintings and sculpture intact.

Dennis provided financial as well as excavational assistance to the Egypt Exploration Society. Through his efforts, funds from Pierpont Morgan were acquired to finance the Deir el-Bahari excavation, and at his urging The Johns Hopkins University donated $265 in 1906/07 and $200 in 1912. As a result of these contributions, the Egypt Exploration Society included the university in the division of material from the excavations of Deir el-Bahari, and, in 1910 to 1913, from the prehistoric sites of Abydos and El Mahasna.

During his seasons in Egypt, Dennis himself acquired several hundred objects, comprising fragments of wall reliefs from the Mentuhotep complex, as well as statuettes, scarabs, palettes, vases, and wooden figurines of various dates of origin. Although his years in the field and his accompanying opportunities to acquire material soon ended, Dennis remained firmly committed to the discipline of Egyptology. He was the author of *Burden of Isis,* published in 1910, and he continued to contribute scholarly articles until his death in 1918.

Dennis bequeathed the bulk of his Egyptian collection to The Johns Hopkins University; today that material forms part of The Johns Hopkins University Archaeological Collection. The remaining Egyptian objects were inherited by members of the Dennis family and are now in the Malden Historical Museum, Malden, Missouri.

Suggestions for Further Reading: Ellen Reeder Williams, *The Archaeological Collection of The Johns Hopkins University* (Baltimore, 1984); *The Baltimore Sun (1 April 1918).*

———*E.R.W.*

---

72   WALL RELIEF FRAGMENT
Egyptian (11th Dynasty), 2134–1991 B.C.
Painted limestone
Greatest preserved height: 5 inches;
    Thickness: 1 ¼ inches
Lent by The Johns Hopkins University, Archaeological
    Collection (no. 2127)

This fragment of delicately carved wall relief represents a woman wearing a long wig and carrying a conical cake. She is preceded by a slender male figure in a mid-length kilt, who pours from a pointed jar. There are traces of hieroglyphs between the figures, and red paint on the legs and torso of the male figure.

    The site at which this relief and the five following artifacts were discovered is discussed by Edouard Naville, et al., in *The XIth Dynasty Temple at Deir el-Bahari,* Egypt Exploration Fund Memoir 28, vols. 1–13 (London, 1907–10).

Provenance: From excavations of the Egypt Exploration Society at the Mentuhotep Temple, Deir el-Bahari, 1905–07

—————————————————————————————————*J.V.C.*

73   WALL RELIEF FRAGMENT
Egyptian (11th Dynasty), 2134–1991 B.C.
Painted limestone

Length: 31 inches; Thickness: 3 ¾ inches
Lent by The Johns Hopkins University, Archaeological
    Collection (no. 9211)

Fragments of scenes of the king hunting and fishing in the marshes were found in the rubbish of the Mentuhotep temple. Here, a crocodile has half-swallowed a fish. The zigzags representing water retain traces of blue paint. The band below the aquatic scene is painted red.

Provenance: From the south wall of the ambulatory surrounding the pyramid of Mentuhotep II, Deir el-Bahari

Selected Reference: Edouard Naville, et al., *The XIth Dynasty Temple at Deir el-Bahari,* (London, 1907), 1:69, pl.16, D.

—————————————————————————————————*J.V.C.*

74   SERVANT FIGURE
Egyptian (11th Dynasty), 2134–1991 B.C.
Painted wood
Height: 4 ¾ inches
Lent by The Johns Hopkins University, Archaeological
    Collection (no. 2471)

A male figure is shown squatting on the ground, with the knees drawn up against the body. The arms, which were pegged into dowels in the shoulder, are missing (except for the upper left arm). A dowel-

hole in the base served to anchor the figure. The body is painted brownish yellow; details of the hair and eyes are painted black. The kilt is white.

    Such figurines, showing servants involved in various domestic activities, were common in Middle Kingdom tombs. The "servants" were needed to keep the household of the next world in order. For this type of figure, see James Henry Breasted, Jr., *Egyptian Servant Statues,* Bollingen Series 13 (Washington, DC, 1948).

Provenance: From the excavations of the Egypt Exploration Society at the Mentuhotep Temple, Deir el-Bahari, 1905–07

—————————————————————————————————*J.V.C.*

75   SERVANT FIGURE
Egyptian (11th Dynasty), 2134–1991 B.C.
Painted wood
Height: 5 ½ inches
Lent by The Johns Hopkins University, Archaeological
    Collection (no. 2470)

This squatting male figure is of the same type as no. 74 and would have served a similar function. The style of the piece is quite different, however, with its elongated, pointed head and very large eyes. The hair is black; the body, yellow; the skirt, white. There is a dowel in the bottom for attaching

73

72

74

79   75   76   77   78

the piece to something. The nose and feet are broken off.

Provenance: From excavations of the Egypt Exploration Society at the Mentuhotep Temple, Deir el-Bahari, 1905–07

—————————————J. V. C.

76   SERVANT FIGURE
Egyptian (11th Dynasty), 2134–1991 B.C.
Painted gesso-covered wood
Height: 5 ⁹⁄₁₆ inches
Lent by The Johns Hopkins University, Archaeological
    Collection (no. 2468)

This wide-eyed figure resembles no. 75 in style. Here, however, the roughly carved wood, with still-preserved vertical groove marks, has been covered with gesso and painted with the usual colors. The pegged-in arms are missing.

Provenance: From excavations of the Egypt Exploration Society at the Mentuhotep Temple, Deir el-Bahari, 1905–07

—————————————J. V. C.

77   SERVANT FIGURE
Egyptian (11th Dynasty), 2134–1991 B.C.
Painted wood
Height: 4 ½ inches
Lent by The Johns Hopkins University, Archaeological
    Collection (no. 2479)

A male figure is seated, with the arms stretched out over the lap. Whatever he was once holding was doweled into the front of the figure. His hair is cut at an oblique angle. The large eyes are outlined by incision. The figure is carved in a style different from nos. 75 and 76. The body has traces of red paint; the skirt, traces of white. The hair is black.

Provenance: From excavations of the Egypt Exploration Society at the Mentuhotep Temple, Deir el-Bahari, 1905–07

—————————————J. V. C.

78   SERVANT FIGURE
Egyptian (11th Dynasty), 2134–1991 B.C.
Wood
Height: 5 ½ inches
Lent by The Johns Hopkins University, Archaeological
    Collection (no. 2474)

This crudely carved figure appears to be seated on the ground, leaning forward with his knees drawn up. There is a large dowel-hole at the base of the torso, for attaching the figure to another object, perhaps a grinding stone. The eyes and mouth are suggested only by a groove across the face. This figure is a particularly primitive example of a servant statuette.

Provenance: From excavations of the Egypt Exploration Society at the Mentuhotep Temple, Deir el-Bahari, 1905–07

—————————————J. V. C.

79   BOAT MODEL
Egyptian (11th Dynasty), 2134–1991 B.C. (?)
Terra-cotta
Height (at prow): 2 ¼ inches; Length: 5 ¼ inches;
    Width: 1 ¾ inches
Lent by The Johns Hopkins University, Archaeological
    Collection (no. 2401)

This hollow model represents an unusual type of short, deep-drafted Egyptian boat, with a square stern. Three cross-beams divide the deck into four parts. The three rear-deck sections are roughly perforated, probably for the insertion of figures. There is a hole amidships for the mast, and one at the stern for the rudder.

Provenance: From excavations of the Egypt Exploration Society at the Mentuhotep Temple, Deir el-Bahari, 1905–07

—————————————J. V. C.

80   MODEL COFFIN
Egyptian (Saitic Period ⟨?⟩), 663–525 B.C.
Painted wood, partly gilt
Height: 24 ¼ inches
Lent by The Johns Hopkins University, Archaeological
    Collection (no. 2911)

This small figure of the the god of the dead, Osiris, wrapped as a mummy, is actually a miniature coffin—probably for an *ushabti* figure. The interior of the piece is roughly carved out to a very shallow depth; the surface of the raw wood is fresh and shows no trace of having contained mummified material. The front and back are pegged together with eight rectangular dowels. The figure wears an elaborate seven-strand collar necklace, a long wig decorated with an *uraeus,* and a beard. Pegged into the top of the head is an *atef* crown, with ostrich feathers and ram's horns.

The long inscription, which runs down the front of the figure, is gilt. Another inscription, on the back of the figure, is written in a yellow-painted band.

The shroud is painted red; the hair, black. A thick coat of gesso, which had been applied to the face before gilding, is in very deteriorated condition. There is a dowel at the feet to peg into a base.

—————————————J. V. C.

80

SAIDIE A. MAY   (1879–1951)
Baltimore

One of Baltimore's most altruistic benefactors was Saidie A. May. Familiar with The Baltimore Museum of Art's holdings and their potential for growth, she developed an art collection that would best complement the public holdings. She presented an extensive collection of ancient, medieval, and Renaissance works of art to the museum in 1933, and subsequently continued to donate to the institution examples of twentieth-century European paintings, drawings, and sculpture.

Mrs. May was one of the five children of Charles Adler, a local shoe manufacturer who patented the elevator heel. She was educated in Baltimore and, developing an interest in art at an early age, she sketched at the Charcoal Club and toured museums and galleries abroad. It was in the early 1920s, while married to Herbert May, a lawyer and department store magnate, that she began to collect the early works, acquiring many from the New York dealer, Joseph Brummer. In the mid-twenties, Mrs. May became acquainted with Mrs. Simon Guggenheim, the collector, and with the American painter, Hans Hoffmann. Her interests then began to shift to the contemporary field. She resided in Paris during the 1930s, studying painting at the Académie Scandinave under Othon Friesz and Charles Dufresne. While in Paris, Mrs. May was particularly drawn to the Surrealist artists André Masson, Joan Miro, Yves Tanguy, and Matta, who are well represented in her collection. She also became interested in American painting, acquiring works by Robert Motherwell and William Baziotes in 1943 and, five years later, a picture by Jackson Pollock.

Although Mrs. May's contributions to art museums are too numerous to cite—institutions in New York, San Diego, and Kansas City all benefited from her generosity—it was The Baltimore Museum of Art that was her chief beneficiary. In addition to contributing her collections, she donated the "Renaissance Room" from Shrewsbury, England, now incorporated into the library, as well as the wing bearing her name, which was originally dedicated to art education, one of her abiding interests.

Suggestion for Further Reading: Jan Harrison Cone, "Saidie A. May Collection," *The Baltimore Museum of Art Record* 3, 1(1972).

———————————————————————————————————————*W.R.J.*

81

81   ROYAL HEAD
Egyptian (4th Dynasty), 2680–2565 B.C.
Diorite
Height: 4 inches
Lent by The Baltimore Museum of Art:
　　Bequest of Saidie A. May

This fine fragment of Old Kingdom sculpture displays pudgy features and bulging eyes, suggesting those of King Mycerinus and his family, who are familiar from their many representations found in the king's valley temple at Gizeh. The beard and the sides of the wig are broken off. The upper left quadrant of the face has been restored.

For good illustrations of the Mycerinus statues, see William Stevenson Smith, *Ancient Egypt as Represented in The Museum of Fine Arts, Boston* (Boston, 1960), 47–49, figs. 22–24.

Provenance: Saidie A. May purchase form Joseph Brummer, New York, 1926

Selected Reference: Jan Harrison Cone, "Saidie A. May Collection," *The Baltimore Museum of Art Record* 3(1972), 9, 20.

———————————————————————————*J.V.C.*

82   RONDEL FROM A SUIT OF ARMOR
Spanish, mid-16th century
Iron inlaid with gold
Diameter: 6 ¾ inches
Lent by The Baltimore Museum of Art:
　　Gift of Saidie A. May

Although a certain amount of sixteenth-century armor was inlaid with gold, few examples have survived. This rondel of russet iron protected the armpit when the arm was lifted. The piece has a raised center and is divided into six gores, each inlaid in gold, with an oval shield surmounted by a casque. There is a border of bryony surrounding the entire design, and the areas are set off with straight, gold lines. The outer border of the rondel is turned over and roped, and there remain seven of the gilt-brass rivets to attach a leather lining, and one to attach the suspension strap.

Provenance: Sir Samuel Rush Meyrick before 1848; Dr. William Meyrick before 1861; Leonard Brassey sale (Christie, Manson, and Woods, 21 February 1922, lot 100); Mrs. Saidie A. May, gift to The Baltimore Museum of Art, 1945. It is possible that the piece was one of those sold by Christie's in 1839 from the Armería Reale, Madrid, though it cannot be identified in the sale catalogue.

Selected Reference: Francis Henry Cripps Day, *A Record of Armour Sales* (London, 1925), 236–37.

—————————————————— *R. H. R.*

ACHILLE-EMILE OTHON, known as OTHON-FRIESZ
French, 1879–1949
83 *Le Lac, Annecy* (1933)
Oil on canvas
19 x 28 inches
Lent by The Baltimore Museum of Art:
　　Bequest of Saidie A. May

Friesz initially trained with Charles Lhuillier, a museum curator in his native Le Havre. In 1898, Friesz went to Paris, where he studied under Léon Bonnat at the Ecole des Beaux-Arts. Eventually, he was attracted to the Post-Impressionists—particularly to Cézanne, Matisse, and Braque. His paintings, which were shown at the salons of the Société des Indépendants and at the Salon d'Automne, also reflected the influences of Fauvism and Expressionism.

Friesz was Saidie May's art instructor at the Académie Scandinave in Paris during the 1930s.

Signed: (at lower left): *E Othon Friesz*; inscribed on reverse: *Le Lac/Annecy 1933/EOF*

Provenance: Saidie A. May, 1934

Selected Reference: Jan Harrison Cone, "Saidie A. May Collection," *The Baltimore Museum of Art Record* 3, 1(1972):59.

—————————————————— *W. R. J.*

82

83

THE CONE SISTERS
Baltimore

In 1898, Etta Cone bought four paintings by the American Impressionist, Theodore Robinson, to enliven the family residence on Eutaw Street. These purchases marked the beginning of what was to become the celebrated Cone Collection.

　　Claribel (1864–1929) and Etta (1870–1949) were two of the twelve children of Herman and Helen Cone, immigrants from Germany. After their marriage in this country, the Cones lived in Jonesboro, Tennessee, until the the early 1870s, when they moved to Baltimore, where Herman opened a wholesale grocery business. By 1888, he was able to retire, leaving responsibility for the family's finances to two sons, Moses and Ceasar [*sic*], who succeeded in organizing a number of southern textile mills into the "Cone Export and Commission Company." In the meantime, both Claribel and Etta graduated from Western Female High School; Claribel then entered the Women's Medical College in Baltimore, while Etta remained at home to tend the household.

　　The fateful friendship between the Cone sisters and the Stein family can be traced to 1892, the year Gertrude Stein and her brother, Leo, came to Baltimore. Members of the same intellectual and social circles, the Steins and the Cones soon became acquainted. Gertrude, who enrolled in medicine at The Johns Hopkins University in 1897, grew particularly close to Claribel, then pursuing postgraduate studies in pathology under the eminent specialist, Dr. William Welch.

　　In 1901, Etta and a couple of companions traveled to Europe and were conducted through the Italian museums by Leo Stein, who shared with them his enthusiasm for Italian painting. Later, in Paris, he also introduced them to Japanese wood-block prints. On another trip, two years later, Etta and Claribel again toured Italy, indulging their tastes for jewelry and textiles, and stopping in Paris, where the Steins had recently taken a studio at 27 rue de Fleurus on the Left Bank, near the Luxembourg Gardens. In 1905/06, the Cone sisters found a nearby apartment at 58 rue Madame. It was there that Etta typed Gertrude's manuscript, *Three Lives.* That winter, Gertrude took Etta to Picasso's studio and encouraged the younger Cone sister to buy a watercolor and an etching for 120 francs ($34). Other members of the Stein family—Gertrude's older brother, Michael, and his wife, Sarah—were responsible for initiating what was to become a lifelong relationship between the Cone sisters and Henri Matisse. Subsequently, the Cones, individually or together, visited Paris on trips abroad, making modest purchases, presumably with the encouragement of the Steins. Although relations between Etta and Gertrude deteriorated after Alice Toklas' arrival at rue de Fleurus, Claribel remained close to the author, and both sisters were, in fact, subjects of Gertrude Stein's verbal portrait, *Two Sisters,* written in 1912 (reprinted by Barbara Pollack, 275–300).

During World War I, the Cones were separated: Etta was at home in Baltimore and Claribel was stranded in Munich. Returning to America in 1920, Claribel found that the family's finances had increased. She was now able to convert an apartment, adjoining that of her sister in the Marlborough Apartments, into a private "museum" for the display of her collections of modern art, antique furniture, and bric-a-brac, including textiles and jewelry. The sisters ate together in Etta's apartment, with a younger brother, Frederick, who was also interested in art and had connecting quarters.

In their postwar travels, the Cones became more ambitious in their acquisitions, frequently buying from Bernheim-Jeune, Matisse's Paris dealer. They were no longer dependent on the Steins for advice, though they frequently assisted Gertrude financially by buying works from her collection when she was strapped for funds. The Cones' reputations as collectors of the first order were assured at the 1926 John Quinn Sale in Paris, at which Claribel paid 101,000 francs for Matisse's controversial masterpiece of 1907, *The Blue Nude.*

The Cones' last trip together was in 1929. They went to Lausanne, where they had prevously dealt with Paul Valloton, hoping that the town's situation on Lake Leman would prove beneficial to Claribel's declining health. Claribel died that September, leaving the art collection to her sister. In her will, Claribel expressed her hope that, should the level of appreciation for modern art in Baltimore improve, Etta would, in turn, bequeath all of their art collection to The Baltimore Museum of Art.

Etta outlived Claribel by twenty years. She scrupulously maintained her sister's "museum," welcoming serious visitors—and, in 1934, she published a catalogue of the combined collections. Etta continued to acquire works, adding historical breadth to the collection through the purchase of such paintings as Gauguin's *Woman with Mango,* Manet's *Lady with a Bonnet,* and Corot's *The Artist's Studio.* In addition, she strengthened the holdings of pictures by Picasso and Matisse, buying a major work by Matisse almost every year.

Upon Etta's death in 1949, The Baltimore Museum of Art received the combined collections. In addition to $100,000 that Claribel had designated for the preservation of the art, Etta allowed $300,000 from her estate to be used in building a wing to house the collection. This money, together with additional funds from the city, enabled the museum to open the Cone Wing in 1955.

Suggestions for Further Reading: *The Cone Collection of Baltimore, Maryland, Catalogue of Paintings–Drawings–Sculpture of the Nineteenth and Twentieth Centuries with a Foreword by George Boas* (Baltimore, 1934); Barbara Pollack, *The Collectors: Dr. Claribel and Miss Etta Cone* (Indianapolis, 1962); Ellen B. Hirschland, "The Cone Sisters and the Stein Family," *Four Americans in Paris,* exh. cat. The Museum of Modern Art (New York, 1970), 75–87.

—*W.R.J.*

HENRI MATISSE
French, 1869–1954
84 *The Pewter Jug* (1916–17)
Oil on canvas
36 ¼ x 25 ⅝ inches
Lent by The Baltimore Museum of Art: The Cone
    Collection formed by Dr. Claribel Cone and
    Miss Etta Cone of Baltimore, Maryland

According to notes taken in 1908 by Sarah Stein, an early patron and pupil of the master, Matisse explained that, "To copy the objects in a still life is nothing; one must render the emotion they awaken in him." Characteristically, in *The Pewter Jug,* he attempted to evoke "the emotion of the ensemble" through the organization of color and the compositional rhythm of the arabesque surface pattern, which reflects the mutual relationships of the objects "all interlaced like a cord or serpent" (Barr, 552).

Signed: *henri Matisse*

Selected References: *The Cone Collection of Baltimore* (Baltimore, 1934), pl.34; Alfred H. Barr, Jr., *Matisse: His Art and His Public* (New York, 1951), 194.

HENRI MATISSE
French, 1869–1954
85 *Reclining Nude I* (1907)
Bronze
Height: 13 ⅞ inches; Length: 19 ¾ inches
Lent by The Baltimore Museum of Art: The Cone
    Collection formed by Dr. Claribel Cone and
    Miss Etta Cone of Baltimore, Maryland

Matisse's pictorial experiments in the expressive potential of color and surface pattern were paralleled after 1901 by his sculptural experiments in the manipulation

—*B.B.*

84

85

of form, for similar expressive purposes. In 1907, Matisse began to work on a reclining nude, but the clay model fell; in frustration, he recorded the idea in the famous *Blue Nude—Souvenir of Biskra* (1907, Cone Collection, The Baltimore Museum of Art). He subsequently resumed work on the sculpture, creating *Reclining Nude I*.

Conceiving the form in terms of the proportionate interrelationship of its composite volumes, Matisse demonstrated two of his theories of sculpture through the tensions and distortions in *Reclining Nude*: "The smaller the bit of sculpture, the more the essentials of form must exist," he postulated, and, as he said to his students in 1908, "The mechanics of construction is the establishment of the oppositions which create the equilibrium of the directions" (Barr, 550–51).

Noting the bold distortions in *Reclining Nude*, Barr observed that, "No sculpture by Matisse is more admirably designed to interest the eye and satisfy the sense of rhythmic *contrapposto* when seen from different points of view" (100). In addition to its visual appeal, the rough modeling of the surface reflects Matisse's belief that a "sculpture must invite us to handle it as an object" (Barr, 551). The importance of this figure as an expression of Matisse's fundamental aesthetic ideals is indicated by its appearance as a motif in numerous works produced during succeeding decades.

Signed: (lower right): *Henri Matisse/6/10*; (rear base): *HM*; (foundry stamp): *Cire/C. Valsuani/Perdue*

Selected References: *The Cone Collection of Baltimore, Maryland* (Baltimore, 1934), pl.120; Alfred H. Barr, Jr., *Matisse: His Art and His Public* (New York, 1951), 94, 100, 140, 179, 205, 217–18; Albert Elsen, *The Sculpture of Matisse* (New York, n.d. ⟨1972?⟩), 72; Gertrude Rosenthal, "Matisse's Reclining Figures," *Baltimore Museum of Art News* 19, 3(February 1956):10–15.

———————————————————— *B.B.*

PABLO PICASSO
Spanish, 1881–1973
86 *Self-Portrait* (1907)
Pen on white wove paper
8 5/16 x 5 7/16 inches
Lent by The Baltimore Museum of Art: The Cone
    Collection formed by Dr. Claribel Cone and
    Miss Etta Cone of Baltimore, Maryland

Having been introduced to the artist and his mistress (Fernande Olivier) by Gertrude Stein, Etta Cone purchased her first paintings by Picasso on 2 November 1905. That Stein forwarded this drawing in a letter to Etta Cone is known from Cone's reply, dated 7 January 1908:

> A funny coincidence—here I am at my desk having come to tell you that it was about time for you to be writing me, and here comes your dear old letter with this delightful sketch of Picasso and Fernando's [sic] wishes. Dey sure am nice folk and I hope to see them in the near future, so thank them for their respects and please give them mine and tell Pablo that Fernando ought to massage his

86

> tummy into shape again. I love his picture for it is just like him.
>
>   (Stein Archives, Yale University)

Inscription: *Bonjour Mlle Cone*; (on verso): *Je vous envoie meilleurs souvenirs Fernand* [sic] *Picasso*

Selected References: *The Cone Collection of Baltimore, Maryland* (Baltimore, 1934), pl.97; *Four Americans in Paris: The Collections of Gertrude Stein and Her Family*, exh. cat., Museum of Modern Art (New York, 1970), 77; V. Carlson, *Picasso Drawings and Watercolors 1899–1907* (Baltimore, 1976), 90–91.

—————————————————— *B.B.*

HENRI MATISSE
French, 1869–1954
87 *Portrait of Etta Cone*   (1933–34)
Charcoal on paper
27 ¾ x 15 ¾ inches
Lent by The Baltimore Museum of Art: The Cone
    Collection formed by Dr. Claribel Cone and
    Miss Etta Cone of Baltimore, Maryland

Etta Cone purchased her first Matisse in 1905 after being introduced to the artist and his work by Michael and Sarah Stein. Like her sister, Dr. Claribel Cone (1864–1929), Etta (1870–1949) maintained a congenial relationship with Matisse and continued to acquire his works throughout her life as a collector.

This vigorous study is one of six sketches produced by the artist at about the same time that he was completing the posthumous drawing of Claribel (Baltimore Museum of Art, Cone Collection), which Etta requested in 1930.

Inscription: (lower right): *Henri Matisse*

Selected References: Alfred H. Barr, Jr., *Matisse: His Art and His Public*, (New York, 1951), 247, pl.95; *The Cone Collection of Baltimore, Maryland* (Baltimore, 1934), pl.96E.

—————————————————— *B.B.*

87

WILLIAM THOMPSON WALTERS   (1819–94)
Baltimore

The only Maryland collection to be treated individually by Edward Strahan in his survey, *The Art Treasures of America* (written in the late 1870s), was that of William T. Walters. Strahan regarded Walters' gallery as "an educator of taste not to be excelled in the New World." The collection, unlike those of so many contemporaries, was not dispersed upon the collector's death, but was left to his son, Henry Walters, who vastly augmented it and finally bequeathed it to Baltimore.

William T. Walters was born in Liverpool, Pennsylvania, a town on the west bank of the Susquehanna River, north of Harrisburg. After training as a civil engineer at the University of Pennsylvania, he worked in the coal and iron industries of central Pennsylvania. In 1841, following the opening of the Tidewater Canal, which linked the interior of Pennsylvania with the Chesapeake Bay, Walters moved to Baltimore, hoping to take advantage of the city's strategic location for commerce. At first, he worked in a commission merchant house dealing in flour and grain, "Hazlehurst and Walters," but by 1850 he had become the head of "W. T. Walters and Co., Importers in Liquors." He married Ellen Harper of Philadelphia, with whom he had three children, Henry (1848–1931), Jennie (1853–1922) and William Thompson (1856–58). The Walters family was listed in the city directories at a sequence of downtown addresses on Fayette, High, and Howard Streets. In 1858 they moved to the fashionable Mount Vernon Place, leasing and eventually purchasing the house at number 65 (later renumbered 5 West).

Walters maintained that he acquired a painting, E. A. Odier's *Bonaparte's Retreat from Moscow*, with the first five dollars he ever earned. After joining The Maryland Historical Society in 1856, he lent a number of pictures to the early exhibitions, including several animal subjects by the local artist, Hugh Newell, and a couple of anonymous copies after the celebrated paintings of Salvator Rosa and Murillo. In the late 1850s, Walters emerged as an influential collector of American art, patronizing not only regional talents—such as the sculptor, William H. Rinehart, and the specialist in American western subjects, Alfred Jacob Miller—but also the foremost national figures, including Asher B. Durand, then president of the National Academy of Design, Frederick E. Church, John F. Kensett, and the portraitist, Charles Loring Elliott.

Walters turned to contemporary European painting at this time, buying J.-L. Gérôme's *Duel After the Masquerade* (no.94), a couple of small genre scenes by the popular leader of the school of Ecouen, P. E. Frère, and several paintings by minor European artists, which had been exhibited in 1859 at the National Academy of Design, New York. With the help of George A. Lucas, a Baltimorean living in Paris, Walters also commissioned a picture from the prominent French figure painter, Hugues Merle, illustrating Nathaniel Hawthorne's *The Scarlet Letter.*

A writer for the *Boston Evening Transcript,* in the earliest account of a visit to the Walters collection (published on 4 March 1861), alluded to pictures by various American and European masters, including Church's *Morning in the Tropics* (no.97). He claimed, however, that the one painting which would "chain our rapt attention till we forget all else about us, and whose power and beauty will haunt our memory long after we have left this chamber of Art" was *The Power of Music to Assuage Grief* by the Belgian, Louis Gallait (no.93).

During the Civil War, the Walters family took an apartment in Paris on the rue de l'Oratoire and traveled through Europe. With Lucas serving as his mentor (see no.90), William Walters visited artists' studios, commissioning works from P. E. Frère, T. Duverger, H. Daumier, J. B. C. Corot, C. Gleyre, and J.-L. Gérôme. A visit to the Crystal Palace, London, in the autumn of 1862 resulted in Walters' developing an abiding interest in oriental ceramics, inspired by the display of Sir Rutherford Alcock's collection. Tragically, Ellen Walters, during the same visit, succumbed to pneumonia.

Back in Baltimore by 1866, William Walters expanded his liquor business, taking as partners John W. McCoy and Joshua P. McCay. Together with another associate, Benjamin F. Newcomer, he began to diversify his interests, investing heavily in a number of southern railroads, which were eventually merged to form the Atlantic Coast Line Railroad, and taking a major role in the development of the Safe Deposit and Trust Company of Baltimore.

During the course of the Civil War, Walters had sold at auction most of his earlier purchases of American art. He now concentrated in three fields: contemporary European painting, the sculpture of A. L. Barye, and oriental ceramics and metalwork. For many foreign purchases, he relied on Lucas to negotiate the transactions, as in the case of Delaroche's replica of the *Hemicycle* from the Ecole des Beaux-Arts, which was whisked out of France during the upheavals of the Commune; in other instances, Walters undertook purchases himself during subsequent visits to Europe. Until 1889, he attended every international exhibition, officiating in Vienna in 1873 as a commissioner of the United States. Opportunities to expand his holdings were also provided by the New York auctions of collections such as August Belmont's (1872), John Taylor Johnston's (1876), John Wolfe's (1882), and Mary Jane Morgan's (1886). The purchase of the Chinese *Peachbloom Vase* (no.101) for $18,000 at the Morgan Sale confirmed William Walters' national reputation as the preeminent collector of oriental ceramics.

The Mount Vernon Place residence was turned into a veritable museum, which eventually included a double parlor in the Pompeian taste, decorated with European porcelains and statuary; a Marie Antoinette-style chamber; an "old Dutch"-style bedroom; a room devoted to the bronzes and watercolors of A. L. Barye; and a small gallery overflowing with fourteen hundred Chinese, and four hundred Japanese, ceramics. A bridge, also jammed with oriental artifacts, connected the back of the house to the large picture gallery built in 1884.

Walters apparently took pride in sharing his collections, as he frequently received guests, either alone or in groups. To raise funds for the Association for the Improvement of the Condition of the Poor, he initiated the practice as early as 1876 of opening the house to the public on a regular basis every spring (February 22, Easter Monday, every Wednesday in February and March, and Wednesdays and Saturdays in April), charging fifty cents admission, with the proceeds being given to the charity. As president of a committee of Americans to erect a monument in honor of Barye on the Île Saint-Louis, Paris, Walters also assumed a major role in organizing a benefit exhibition held at the American Art Association, New York, from 15 November 1889 to 15 January 1890. In addition to Barye's works, the exhibition included one hundred paintings by members of "the phalanx of 1830"—Géricault, Delacroix, Corot, Daubigny, Decamps, Millet, and Rousseau—thus providing New Yorkers with their first thorough exposure to the art of that generation.

In much the same spirit, William Walters embarked on a program of publications pertaining to his collections.

A modest catalogue of the paintings appeared in 1878, succeeded by a series of more elaborate publications issued intermittently after 1884, documenting the gradual growth of the collection. In addition, Walters produced a booklet, *Oriental Porcelain* (1884), pertaining to the ceramic collection, as well as several books pertaining to Barye and his contemporaries. The two most ambitious publishing ventures were completed after Walters' death: in 1895, *Notes: Critical and Biographical: Collection of W. T. Walters* appeared, with essays by Richard B. Gruelle and typography designed by Bruce Rogers, and in 1897, the multi-volumed *Oriental Ceramic Art* was published, with a text by S. W. Bushell and chromolithographs by Prang and Company.

Suggestions for Further Reading: Edward Strahan (Earl Shinn), *The Art Treasures of America, being the choicest works of art in the public and private collections of America* (Philadelphia, c.1878), 81–94; Dorothy Miner, "The Publishing Ventures of A Victorian Connoisseur, A sidelight of William T. Walters," *Papers of the Bibliographical Society of America* 57, (1963):271–311; Denys Sutton, "Connoisseur's Haven," *Apollo* 84, 58 (December 1966):2–13; *The Diary of George A. Lucas: An American Art Agent in Paris, 1857–1909,* transcribed with introduction by Lilian M. C. Randall, 2 vols. (Princeton, 1979).

—*W. R. J.*

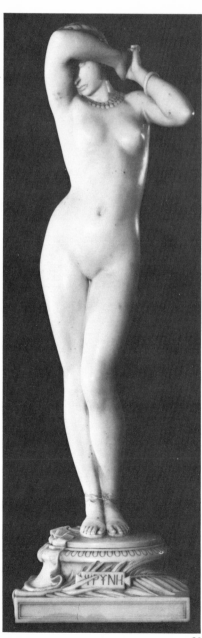

88

JEAN-ALEXANDRE-JOSEPH FALGUIÈRE
French, 1831–1900
88 *Phryne* (1868)
Marble
Height (with base): 31 inches
Lent by The Maryland Institute, College of Art;
    George A. Lucas Collection

Among the most notable sculptors of the last third of the nineteenth century, Falguière exhibited at every Salon from 1863 to 1899, and participated regularly in the Expositions Universelles. He drew much official recognition, attaining the rank of *commandeur* of the Legion of Honor in 1889, and attracted many students to his atelier.

As a subject, Phryne, a Greek courtesan of the fourth century B.C. who is reputed to have served as a model for both Praxiteles and Apelles, provided nineteenth-century artists with the opportunity of displaying an idealized nude, a notable example being Jean-Léon Gérôme's *Phryne before the Areopagus* (Hamburg, Kunsthalle). The success of this picture was such that Gérôme's students replicated the figure of the courtesan in their *surtout de table* for the fête celebrating the painter's nomination to the Institut de France in 1865. Gérôme's dealer, Goupil, commissioned from Falguière a plaster version of the painter's Phryne, which was edited in bronze in 1868 and was also produced in ivory and silver versions. In the late winter and spring of 1868 Falguière himself carved three marble statuettes of Phryne. These were cited by G. A. Lucas, who purchased the third example at Goupil's that November.

Inscription: *A Falguiere,* ΨPYNH, *J L Gerome*

Provenance: Goupil et Cie., to G. A. Lucas, 3 December 1868

Selected References: Fanny Field Hering, *Gérôme* (New York, 1892), 219; *The Diary of George A. Lucas: An American Art Agent in Paris, 1857-1909,* transcribed with introduction by Lilian M.C. Randall, 2 vols. (Princeton, 1979), 2:261, 265, 268–70, 282–84.

—*B. B.*

ANTOINE-LOUIS BARYE
French, 1796–1875
89 *The Walking Lion* (1865)
Silver
Height: 13 ½ inches; Length: 25 ¼ inches
The Walters Art Gallery (27.167)

Barye's most famous composition, *The Walking Lion,* was first cast in bronze in 1835/36. This unique silver version was commissioned in 1865 at a cost of ten thousand francs for presentation to the winner of horse races at Longchamps on 30 April 1865. The winning horse, "La Fille de l'Air," was owned by the Count de Lagrange, who received his trophy directly from the emperor Napoleon III. Following the count's death in 1884, the silver lion was sold at auction. George A. Lucas acquired the piece for William T. Walters the following year. To confirm its authenticity, he showed it to Madame Barye, who noted an extra bar of silver that her husband had attached to the base in order to utilize all the metal that had been supplied for the commission.

Signed: *BARYE*

Provenance: Count de Lagrange; acquired by G. A. Lucas for W. T. Walters, 30 January 1865 for 10,500 francs, from the Paris dealer Montaignac

Selected Reference: Stuart Pivar, "Barye's Silver Lion," *Bulletin of The Walters Art Gallery* 22, 2 (November 1969).

—*W. R. J.*

89

90

LEON-JOSEPH-FLORENTIN BONNAT
French, 1833–1922
90   *Portrait of George Aloysius Lucas*   (1885)
Oil on canvas
50 ⅞ x 36 ½ inches
The Walters Art Gallery (37.759)

In 1857, George Lucas (1824–1909) left
Baltimore for Paris. Remaining abroad, he
served as a consultant and agent for a num-
ber of American collectors, including Frank
Frick, John W. Garrett, Charles J. M. Eaton,
J. Stricker Jenkins, and William and Henry
Walters, all of Baltimore.

   William T. Walters commissioned this
work from the fashionable portraitist of
France's Third Republic to adorn the "Barye
Room," which he opened in his Mount Vernon Place house in 1885.

   George A. Lucas left his collection of
nineteenth-century prints, paintings, and
sculpture to Henry Walters, who in turn
presented it to The Maryland Institute.
Most of the collection is now deposited in
The Baltimore Museum of Art.

Signed and Dated: *Ln Bonnat / 1885*

Selected Reference: For a discussion and listing of exhibitions
and bibliography, see W. R. Johnston, *The Nineteenth Century
Paintings in the Walters Art Gallery,* (Baltimore, 1982), 125,
no.139.

——————————————— *W. R. J.*

FERDINAND VICTOR EUGENE DELACROIX
French, 1798–1863
91   *Christ on the Cross*   (1846)
Oil on canvas
31 ½ x 25 ¼ inches
The Walters Art Gallery (37.62)

91

Parallels have often been noted between Delacroix's paintings of the Crucifixion and those of the seventeenth-century master, Peter Paul Rubens. This work is one of the most frequently cited versions of the subject to which Delacroix turned on numerous occasions throughout his career.

William T. Walters was particularly pleased to obtain this painting, which had been included in the *Cent Chefs-d'Oeuvre,* a celebrated exhibition of a hundred purported masterpieces, held in Paris in 1883.

Signed and Dated: (lower right): *Eug. Delacroix 1846*

Provenance: Purchased by W. T. Walters from the Paris dealer Montaignac in May 1886, for 29,500 francs

Selected Exhibitions: Salon, Paris, 1847, no.459; *Cent Chefs-d'Oeuvre,* Exposition Universelle, Paris, 1855, no.2909; Galerie Georges Petit, Paris, 1883, no.27

Selected References: Alfred Robaut and Ernest Chesneau, *L'Oeuvre complet de Eugène Delacroix* (Paris, 1885), 258, no.986; W. R. Johnston, *The Nineteenth Century Paintings in the Walters Art Gallery* (Baltimore, 1982), 45–46, no.14.

———————————————— *W.R.J.*

MARIANO FORTUNY Y MARSAL
Spanish, 1838–74
92　*An Ecclesiastic*　(1874)

92

94

93

Oil on panel
7 ½ x 5 ⅛ inches
The Walters Art Gallery (37.150)

Fortuny, a Catalan painter, worked in Rome and in Spain. Through the promotional endeavors of his dealer, Goupil, he acquired an international clientele and was particularly admired by American collectors.

Signed: *Fortuny 74* (?)

Provenance: Acquired by W. T. Walters between 1878 and 1884

Selected Reference: For discussion and listing of exhibitions and bibliography, see W. R. Johnston, *The Nineteenth Century Paintings in the Walters Art Gallery* (Baltimore, 1982), 178, no.216.

———————————————— *W.R.J.*

LOUIS GALLAIT
Belgian, 1810–87
93　*The Power of Music to Assuage Grief*
　　　(before 1861)
Oil on panel
22 ½ x 17 ⅟₁₆ inches
The Walters Art Gallery (37.134)

Two destitute young musicians have collapsed beside a tomb on the wayside. The youth attempts to assuage the girl's grief with his music. A replica of a larger work in the Royal Museum, Brussels, this painting was one of the first European works to be purchased by William T. Walters.

In an early review of the Walters collection published in the *Boston Evening Transcript,* 4 March 1861, the correspondent wrote:

> We come at once to a picture which will chain our rapt attention till we forget all

else about us, and whose power and beauty will haunt our memory long after we have left this chamber of Art.

Signed: (at lower left): *Louis Gallait*

Provenance: Acquired by W. T. Walters before 1861

Selected Reference: For discussion and listing of exhibitions and bibliography, see W. R. Johnston, *The Nineteenth Century Paintings in the Walters Art Gallery* (Baltimore, 1982), 159–61, no.166.

———————————————— *W.R.J.*

JEAN-LÉON GÉRÔME
French, 1824–1904
94　*The Duel After the Masquerade*　(after 1857)
Oil on canvas
15 ⅜ x 22 ⅛ inches
The Walters Art Gallery (37.51)

Gérôme, a painter of historic and ethnographic pictures, was admired for his objective realism. As professor of painting at the French state art school, the Ecole des Beaux-Arts, he exerted widespread influence on his many pupils, who were of French and other nationalities. Americans who studied with him included Thomas Eakins, Frederick Bridgeman, and Edwin Lord Weeks.

This painting, a replica of one painted for the duc d'Aumale in 1857, shows the mortally wounded Pierrot falling into the arms of the duc de Guise. The subject, a duel at dawn in the Bois de Boulogne on the outskirts of Paris, was inspired by an actual incident.

The purchase of this painting in 1859 marked a turning point in the evolution of the Walters collection. Thereafter, the emphasis was on European rather than American art.

Signed: (at lower left): *J. L. GEROME*

Provenance: Purchased by W. T. Walters at the National Academy of Design, 1859, for $2,500.

Selected Exhibition: *Collection of English and French Paintings,* Second Annual Exhibition, National Academy of Design, New York, 1859

Selected Reference: W. R. Johnston, *The Nineteenth Century Paintings in the Walters Art Gallery,* (Baltimore, 1982), 101–02, no.105.

———————————————— *W.R.J.*

The location of this scene has been identified as the banks of the river Touques in Normandy.

Signed and Dated: (at bottom left): *C Troyon 1851*

Provenance: Purchased at the G. Viot Sale, Paris, 1886, no.9, for 71,000 francs

Selected Exhibitions: *Cent Chefs-d'Oeuvre*, Galerie Georges Petit, Paris, 1883, no.87; Barye Monument Association, American Art Galleries, New York, 1889/90, no.533

Selected References: Albert Wolff, *Cent Chefs-d'Oeuvre* (New York, 1885), 72; W. R. Johnston, *The Nineteenth Century Paintings in the Walters Art Gallery* (Baltimore, 1982), 66, no.47.

———————————————————— *W. R. J.*

FREDERICK EDWIN CHURCH
American, 1826–1900
97 *Morning in the Tropics* (c.1858)
Oil on canvas
8 ¼ x 14 inches
The Walters Art Gallery (37.147)

Church donated this landscape to the National Academy of Design, for an auction held on 20 December 1858 to benefit the widow of the artist William Ranney (1813–57). William T. Walters paid $555 for the picture, a sum said to have been the highest ever given in the country for so small a landscape. Despite its size, *Morning in the Tropics* was one of Church's better-known works; it was engraved and frequently copied.

Provenance: National Academy of Design, New York, 20 December 1858, to W. T. Walters for $555

———————————————————— *W. R. J.*

95

JEAN-LOUIS ERNEST MEISSONIER
French, 1815–91
95 *1814* (1862)
Oil on panel
12 ¾ x 9 ½ inches
The Walters Art Gallery (37.52)

One of William T. Walters' favorite paintings, which he displayed separately mounted on an easel in his early gallery, was this painting of Napoleon. John Ruskin, a former owner of the picture, identified the scene as Napoleon on the Chausée de Vitry just after the 1814 battle of Arcis-sur-Aube.

Signed and Dated: (lower right): *E* [conjoined] *Meissonier 1862*

Provenance: Prince Napoleon, Sale, 4 April 1868, no.18; J. Ruskin, Sale, 3 June 1882, no.111; Defoer Sale, 22 May 1886 to W. T. Walters for 128,000 francs.

Selected Exhibition: International Exhibition, London, 1862, no.190

Selected Reference: For discussion and listing of exhibitions and bibliography, see W. R. Johnston, *The Nineteenth Century Paintings in the Walters Art Gallery* (Baltimore, 1982), 112–13, no.117.

———————————————————— *W. R. J.*

CONSTANT TROYON
French, 1810–65
96 *Cattle Drinking* (1851)
Oil on panel
30 ⅞ x 20 ⅜ inches
The Walters Art Gallery (37.59)

Troyon's practice of including farm animals in his landscapes began in the early 1840s and was reinforced in 1847 by a trip to the Netherlands and Belgium, where he was particularly impressed by the animal subjects of Paul Potter and Albert Cuyp, both seventeenth-century artists.

96

97

98

WILLIAM HENRY RINEHART
American, 1825–74
98 *Model for the Walters family tomb,
Greenmount Cemetery* (1865)
Plaster
Height: 69 inches
Lent by The Peabody Institute

After a visit in 1862 to the Crystal Palace, London, Mrs. William T. Walters succumbed to pneumonia. In 1865, her husband commissioned from Rinehart this female figure, otherwise known as *Love Reconciled with Death.* In 1866, in Munich, the model was cast in bronze; it was erected the following year in Greenmount Cemetery, Baltimore.

Rinehart had been on exceptionally close terms with Ellen Walters and the Walters children, and the monument was reputed to have been "the saddest, but sweetest, duty he ever had to perform."

Provenance: The plaster listed as "Girl Strewing Flowers Monumental figure life-size" was transferred following the artist's death from his studio in Rome to The Peabody Institute.

Selected Reference: William Sener Rusk, *William Henry Rinehart* (Baltimore, 1939), 37–38.

——————————————— *W. R. J.*

WILLIAM HENRY RINEHART
American, 1825–74
99 *Bust of W. T. Walters* (1866/67)
Marble
Height: 21 ½ inches
The Walters Art Gallery (28.9)

During a return visit to Baltimore in 1866, Rinehart produced the model for this bust of William Walters, his friend and principal patron. The marble was carved following Rinehart's return to Rome.

Walters commissioned a number of works from this sculptor, who began his career working in the stone-yard of Baughman and Bevan on the site of what is now The Peabody Institute, Baltimore.

Provenance: W. T. Walters commissioned the bust in 1866

Selected Reference: William Sener Rusk, *William Henry Rinehart* (Baltimore, 1939), 17, 64.

——————————————— *W. R. J.*

GILBERT STUART
American, 1755–1828
100 *Portrait of James David Barry*
Oil on canvas
38 x 34 inches
Lent by The Art Museum, Princeton University,
    Bequest of Mrs. Vanderbilt Webb

After rather checkered beginnings in the American Northeast and in Edinburgh, Scotland, Stuart entered the London studio of Benjamin West as a student and emerged as West's principal assistant. Stuart launched an independent career in 1781. Although he received numerous commissions, he accumulated debts and left portraits unfinished, finally retiring to Dublin, Ireland, where he repeated the unfortunate process. In 1792 he returned to America, becoming the principal portrait painter of the Federal period.

Barry was born in Ireland and came to America in the late eighteenth century as the British consul. He lived in New York and in Washington, where in 1797 he built a mansion, which was designed by James Hoban, architect of the White House. Barry was active in municipal affairs and was a friend of George Washington (L. D. Hutchinson, *The Anacostia Story: 1608–1930* (Washington, DC, 1977), 27–28).

Between 1876 and 1887, this portrait was featured in Walters' picture gallery.

Provenance: Commissioned by James Barry; Robert Barry, Baltimore; C. M. Leupp collection; John Taylor Johnston, Sale, 19 December 1876, lot 55; purchased by William T. Walters for $560; to Samuel P. Avery before 1887; purchased by William T. Osborn, New York; by descent to Mrs. Vanderbilt Webb

Selected References: George C. Mason, *The Life and Works of Gilbert Stuart* (New York, 1879), 133–34; *Catalogue of the Collection of William T. Walters* (c.1878, 17; 1884, no.24).

——————————————— *B. B.*

101 PEACHBLOOM VASE
Chinese, (Qing dynasty/Kangxi reign), after
    1682–1722
Porcelain, peachbloom glaze
Height: 8 inches
The Walters Art Gallery (49.155)

"Peachbloom" is an American term for the red-based glaze which, when fired, becomes mottled with spots of pink, green, and russet. It was one of the transmutational glazes developed at the imperial kilns at Jingdezhen, and was employed in making a

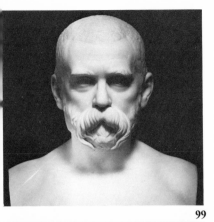

99

100

mained reticent regarding subsequent purchases, rightly feeling that the appreciation of art objects becomes muddled when their value is translated into dollars.

Interest in the transmutational glazes of the Kangxi period faded in the twentieth century, partly because of a growing fascination with wares of earlier times. Recent studies based on the production records of Jingdezhen have enabled scholars to distinguish originals from later imitations and to reappraise the elegance of the transmutational glazes. The famous *Peachbloom Vase,* as well as the other examples in the Walters collection, are indeed among the finest specimens in existence.

Provenance: "I Wang-ye, a Mandarin Prince"; Mrs. Mary J. Morgan (her sale, American Art Association, 3 March 1886, lot 341): acquired at the Morgan sale by William T. Walters

Selected Reference: S. W. Bushell, *Oriental Ceramic Art* (New York, 1980, orig. ed. New York, 1896), 377, pl. 111

—————————————————— *L. H. A.*

102   BRUSH WASHER
Chinese (Qing dynasty/Kangxi reign), after
     1682–1722
Porcelain, peachbloom glaze
Diameter: 4 ¹¹⁄₁₆ inches
The Walters Art Gallery (49.685)

See no. 101.

Signed: *Kangxi*

—————————————————— *L. H. A.*

103   CIRCULAR BOX FOR SEAL VERMILION
     (YIN SE HO)
Chinese (Qing dynasty/Kangxi reign),
     after 1682–1722
Porcelain, peachbloom glaze
Diameter: 2 ¹³⁄₁₆ inches
The Walters Art Gallery (49.153 A, B)

See no. 101.

—————————————————— *L. H. A.*

104   WRITER'S WATER VESSEL *(T'AI-PO TSUN)*
Chinese (Qing dynasty/Kangxi reign), after
     1682–1722
Porcelain, peachbloom glaze
Diameter: 5 inches
The Walters Art Gallery (49.692)

Henry Walters retained his father's interest in oriental ceramics, and purchased this piece to complete the collection with an example of the fourth shape typical of peachbloom wares (see no. 101).

very limited number of small, exquisite objects intended for the writing desks of an exclusive clientele that included only nobles and high government officials.

By the middle of the nineteenth century, American collectors had become familiar with the rare peachbloom glaze. Among those objects acquired directly from a Chinese collection was the flawless flower vase belonging to Mary Morgan, the widow of the shipping magnate, Charles Morgan. By the 1880s, William T. Walters had become one of the premier collectors of monochrome and mottled glazed porcelains, and he enthusiastically sought the one object having a "world wide reputation of being the finest specimen of its class in existence." By the time it was auctioned on 8 March 1886, newspaper articles and even a poem published in *The New York Times* had made the peachbloom vase a household term. The controversy regarding its merits intensified when it became known that Walters had acquired it for the unprecedented sum of $18,000. Disturbed by the journalistic sensationalism, Walters re-

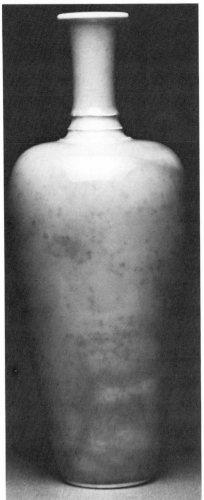

101

102   **103**

104

Signed: *Kangxi*

Provenance: Purchased by Henry Walters from Yamanaka, 25 January 1917

—————————————————— *L.H.A.*

105 BOX FOR STORAGE OF DOCUMENTS
(RYOSHI-BAKO)
Japanese (Edo period), 18th–19th century
Black and gold lacquer
Height: 6 ¼ inches; Length: 16 ½ inches;
　　　Width: 16 ½ inches
The Walters Art Gallery (67.188)

This large box is decorated with scenery, including houses, pine trees, blossoming cherry trees, and scattered *aoi* crests (the badge of the Togukawa family).

— *L.H.A.*

106 BOX FOR INKSTONE AND WRITING
IMPLEMENTS *(SUZURI-BAKO)*
Height: 1 ⅞ inches; Length: 8 ¹³⁄₁₆ inches;
　　　Width: 9 ¹¹⁄₁₆ inches
The Walters Art Gallery (67.18)

Decoration matches no.105

— *L.H.A.*

105

106

107

108

107 OCTAGONAL BOX
Japanese, probably 19th century
Copper, gold, and silver
Height: 1 ⅞ inches; Length: 3 ¾ inches
The Walters Art Gallery (53.91)

The cover is decorated in relief, partially in gold and silver, showing a magician calling forth a fairy. The interior is lined in silver.

Signed: Seal mark, and two-character signature at the right

— *L.H.A.*

108 THREE-CLAWED DRAGON
Japanese
Silver (claws, eyes) and gold (tongue)
Height: 6 ⅝ inches; Length: 9 ½ inches
The Walters Art Gallery (57.1188)

Marks: Inscription on two plaques and seal mark on bottom

109 KOZUKA (KNIFE HANDLE)
Japanese
Alloy of copper, silver, and traces of gold and iron
　　　(shibuichi)
Length: 3 ¹⁵⁄₁₆ inches
The Walters Art Gallery (51.847)

109

110

111

112

113

114

115

116

This work is decorated with flowers in gold, copper, silver, and *shibuichi* relief.

110 KOZUKA (KNIFE HANDLE)
Japanese
Copper
Length: 3 ¹⁵⁄₁₆ inches
The Walters Art Gallery (51.848)

The decorations represent kingfishers and other birds, in relief, on a tree engraved into the metal.

111 KOZUKA (KNIFE HANDLE)
Japanese
Alloy of copper, silver, and traces of gold and iron
　　　(shibuichi)
Length: 3 ¹⁵⁄₁₆ inches
The Walters Art Gallery (51.841)

The object is decorated with a clam (in gold), copper seaweed, and small houses and temples outlined in the background.

Verso: Five-character inscription

117   118   119

120   *KABUTO* (HELMET)
Japanese
Iron
Length: 12 ⅜ inches
The Walters Art Gallery (51.607)

The crest represents a dragonfly.

Provenance: Bunkio Matsuki (?)

112   *KOZUKA* (KNIFE HANDLE)
Japanese
Copper and silver relief
Length: 3 ¹³⁄₁₆ inches
The Walters Art Gallery (51.844)

The view, in silver relief, is of Mt. Fuji.

Verso: Gold, with two long inscriptions

116   *KOZUKA* (KNIFE HANDLE)
Japanese
Copper, decorated with copper and gold
Length: 3 ¹³⁄₁₆ inches
The Walters Art Gallery (51.843)

The figure is Fu Ku-roku-ju.

121   COVERED CYLINDRICAL JAR
Japanese (Hirado ware), 19th century
Porcelain
Height: 6 ¾ inches
The Walters Art Gallery (49.1542)

The jar is decorated in underglaze blue with
morning glories and a section of reed fence.
A small dragon, in relief on the cover, serves
as a handle.

113   *KOZUKA* (KNIFE HANDLE)
Japanese
Copper with silver, gold, and copper inlay
Length: 3 ¹³⁄₁₆ inches
The Walters Art Gallery (51.845)

The design of basket and vines is set against
an incised pattern of mounds of earth.

Verso: Inlaid strips of copper and gold

117   *TSUBA* (SWORDGUARD)
Japanese
Copper and gold
Length: 2 ⅞ inches
The Walters Art Gallery (51.274)

The floral decoration represents chrysan-
themums.

114   *KOZUKA* (KNIFE HANDLE)
Japanese
Alloy of copper, silver, and traces of gold and iron
    (*shibuichi*)
Length: 3 ¹³⁄₁₆ inches
The Walters Art Gallery (51.846)

The relief decoration shows birds perched
on a *shibuichi* dipper, in a field with a stack
of hay (in gold).

118   *TSUBA* (SWORDGUARD)
Japanese
Copper and enamel
Length: 3 ³⁄₁₆ inches
The Walters Art Gallery (51.168)

The scattered kiri leaves are in translucent
green. Taoist symbols are included in the
decoration.

Marks: Seal marks on both sides and inscriptions around the hilt
opening

120

115   *KOZUKA* (KNIFE HANDLE)
Japanese
Copper, decorated with different metals
Length: 3 ¹³⁄₁₆ inches
The Walters Art Gallery (51.842)

Hotei, the monk of the hempen bag, is
shown in relief.

119   *TSUBA* (SWORDGUARD)
Japanese
Copper, inlaid in gold
Diameter: 3 ¹⁄₁₆ inches
The Walters Art Gallery (51.155)

The design represents clouds in diaper
work, a screen, and a vase of flowers.

121

122

122 VASE

Japanese (Kyoyaki), 19th century

Porcelain, glazed black, with enamel

Height: 11 ⅜ inches

The Walters Art Gallery (49.1882)

The vase imitates the style of the famous potter, Ninsei, who was active during the mid-seventeenth century. The enameled decoration represents peonies (?) and peacock feather ornaments. *Fu*-dog handles are included.

---

123 VASE

Japanese (Satsuma ware), 19th century

Faience, with finely crackled glaze

Height: 12 ⁵⁄₁₆ inches

The Walters Art Gallery (49.2190)

The lip and lower part of the vase are enameled blue; a myriad of maple leaves is colored green, red, and gold; at the top are scudding clouds in gold.

123

HENRY WALTERS   (1848–1931)

Baltimore

The state's preeminent art collector was a Baltimorean in absentia. Though most of his adult life was spent elsewhere, Henry Walters maintained his collection in a personal gallery in the city of his birth.

Henry's early education at Loyola College was interrupted by the Civil War. He continued his studies at a lycée in Paris and subsequently attended Georgetown University, graduating in 1869 and receiving an M.A. degree in 1871. To prepare for a career in railroading, he pursued studies at the Lawrence Scientific School, Harvard University, until 1873, obtaining a *nunc pro tunc* B.S. degree in 1906.

Before joining his father's railroad, Henry Walters worked in the engineering corps of the Valley Railroad of Virginia, as well as for the Pittsburgh and Connellsville line. By 1889, he had become vice-president and general manager of the Atlantic Coast Line. Later, he served as its president and, at the time of his death, was chairman of the board and chief shareholder. Under his leadership, the Atlantic Coast Line gained control of other lines, among them the Louisville and Nashville and the vast Plant system, creating one of the country's largest rail networks.

In Baltimore, Henry Walters continued the family association with the Safe Deposit and Trust Company, becoming a director immediately after his father's death, serving as vice-president from 1900 to 1915, and thereafter acting as chairman of the board.

When not traveling, Henry Walters divided his time among several locations, the railroads' headquarters in Wilmington, North Carolina; New York; and Newport, Rhode Island. Owning no property apart from his father's residence on Mount Vernon Place, he was invariably the houseguest of his lifelong friends, Mr. and Mrs. Pembroke Jones. Although visits to Baltimore were usually confined to monthly board meetings of the Safe Deposit and Trust Company, followed by stops at the art gallery, Henry Walters retained his ties with the city: in 1900, he contributed a system of public bath houses for the core of the city; in 1905, he donated to The Maryland Institute the art collection that he had inherited from George

A. Lucas; he also funded the Department of Art as Applied to Medicine and a chair in zoology for The Johns Hopkins University. In addition, Henry continued his father's practice of raising money for the Association for the Improvement of the Condition of the Poor, with annual showings of the family's art collection.

In New York, Walters served as trustee and vice-president of The Metropolitan Museum of Art, as trustee of the New York Public Library, and a member of the Grolier Club. Among the many institutions to benefit from his generosity were the Wadsworth Atheneum, Hartford, Connecticut; Georgetown Preparatory School, Washington, DC, for which he erected a main building in the name of the class of 1869; and the American Academy in Rome. As an inveterate Francophile, he maintained a military hospital at Passy during World War I, receiving in recognition for this service the Medaille de la Reconnaissance and the order of the Legion of Honor.

Given the strong bond between the Walters father and son, and Henry's participation in many of William's forays into the art market, it is not surprising that the younger Walters adhered at first to collecting aims set by his father. Although Henry continued to buy pictures by the artists his father had admired (among them Gérôme and Meissonier) years after such works had fallen out of fashion, the son was also able to enrich the collection with nineteenth-century works by such masters as Géricault, Delacroix, and Ingres, as well as by the Impressionists.

It soon became apparent, however, that the younger Walters' goals for the collection were much more ambitious. At the age of fifty, he began a trend which in the three succeeding decades would result in a collection of more than twenty-two thousand works, illustrating the range of artistic creativity over four millennia. As early as 1893, at the Chicago World's Fair, he is believed to have obtained some ancient Near Eastern cylinder seals from Dikran Kelekian, and four years later, he was acquiring Americana, poetry, and incunabula from George H. Richmond. At the W. W. Forman Sale of June 1899, Walters bought his first Etruscan and Roman bronzes. Though he was not interested in modern painting, Walters sought out exceptional examples of contemporary decorative arts—including some bibelots he saw in Fabergé's St. Petersburg shop in 1900, during a cruise on his yacht *Narada*, as well as a number of pieces of fabulous jewelry shown by René Lalique at the St. Louis World's Fair in 1904.

The purchase that was to transform the collection was made in 1902—Walters bought the contents of the Accoramboni Palace on Rusticucci Square, Rome. This collection had belonged to Don Marcello Massarenti, Assistant Almoner to the Holy See under Popes Leo XIII and Pius X, and comprised more than 1,540 works, including 500 late medieval, Renaissance, and Baroque paintings, numerous examples of Renaissance sculpture and decorative arts, and a distinguished array of antiquities—among them, seven marble sarcophagi that had been discovered in 1884 in a tomb near the via Salaria, Rome. To transport the collection to America, a steamship (the *Minterne*) had to be chartered, and to house the many works of art in Baltimore, a building had to be erected. The new gallery, with its interior modeled after Bartolomeo Bianco's Palazzo dell'Università, Genoa, was designed by William Adams Delano of the firm of Delano and Aldrich and was opened to visitors in 1909.

Meanwhile, Walters expanded his holdings with medieval manuscripts purchased from Léon Gruel of Paris, with Near Eastern ceramics, manuscripts, and textiles from Dikran Kelekian, with Roman sculpture from the Madame E. Warnek Sale of 1905, and with other antiquities from C. S. E. Canessa. Continuing his practice of acquiring collections in toto, he bought Leo S. Olschki's entire stock of more than a thousand incunabula in 1905, with the stipulation that the Florentine dealer provide an illustrated catalogue of the works.

Although the new gallery was quickly filled, the pace of Walters' acquisitions never waned, except during the war years. Determined to assemble an all-encompassing collection, he showed remarkable initiative and independence of judgment in purchasing Coptic ivories, Sasanian silver, Hunnish jewelry, and works in countless other fields. More conventional was his taste for the arts of eighteenth-century France, which was most noticeable in the 1920s, following his marriage in 1922 to Sarah Wharton Jones, the widow of Pembroke Jones. Superb examples of furniture were gathered, including pieces signed by Jacques Dubois, David Roentgen, Jean Henri Riesener, and Bernard II van Riesenburgh, but these remained in the New York apartment and were ultimately dispersed at auction. A major collection of Sèvres porcelains, assembled by E. M. Hodgkins in the late nineteenth century, was purchased in its entirety in 1928 from Arnold Seligmann, Rey and Company, and was sent to the Walters gallery.

It was not until his will was read, following his death in 1931, that the younger Walters' intentions for the disposition of the collection were divulged. He bequeathed the family holdings to the Mayor and City Council of Baltimore for the benefit of the people, and provided for the collection's maintenance with an endowment of one-quarter of his estate.

Suggestions for Further Reading: The Walters Art Gallery issue, *The Art Bulletin* 18, 2 (June 1936); The Walters Art Gallery issues, *Apollo* 84, 58 (December 1966) and 100, 153 (November 1974); Richard H. Randall, Jr., "A French Quartet," *Bulletin of The Walters Art Gallery* 23, 3 (December 1970).

— W. R. J.

---

124 STATUETTE
Egyptian (Middle Kingdom), 2040–1786 B.C.
Serpentine
Height: 12 inches
The Walters Art Gallery (22.203)

This very fine example of private funerary sculpture, which represents a man in a suspended kilt, was famous long before it came

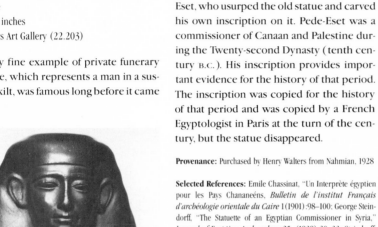

to The Walters Art Gallery. The inscription on the back pillar is a dedication by a Pede-Eset, who usurped the old statue and carved his own inscription on it. Pede-Eset was a commissioner of Canaan and Palestine during the Twenty-second Dynasty (tenth century B.C.). His inscription provides important evidence for the history of that period. The inscription was copied for the history of that period and was copied by a French Egyptologist in Paris at the turn of the century, but the statue disappeared.

Provenance: Purchased by Henry Walters from Nahmian, 1928

Selected References: Emile Chassinat, "Un Interprète égyptien pour les Pays Chananeéns, *Bulletin de l'institut Français d'archéologie orientale du Caire* 1 (1901):98–100; George Steindorff, "The Statuette of an Egyptian Commissioner in Syria," *Journal of Egyptian Archaeology* 25, (1939):30–33; Steindorff, *Catalogue of the Egyptian Sculpture in The Walters Art Gallery* (Baltimore, 1946), no.145, pl.25.

— J. V. C.

---

125 FACE OF A STAMP SEAL
Hittite, 1400 B.C.
Silver
Diameter: 1 ⅝ inches
The Walters Art Gallery (57.1512)

This inscribed face of a stamp seal is one of the most famous and important documents in the ancient collections of The Walters Art Gallery. Around the outer edge are the wedge-shaped signs of the cuneiform script. They give the name of the owner of the seal, "Targasna-Tiwa, King of Mera." Scattered around the figure of the king in the center of the design are Hittite hieroglyphic signs. The piece was of major importance in deciphering the hieroglyphs, for it was until the 1930s the only known document in which the mysterious signs were accompanied by a readable inscription. The piece has been known since 1863, when it was brought to the British Museum, which made electrotypes of the seal but did not buy it.

Provenance: M. Alexander Jovanoff, Istanbul, 1860; purchased by Henry Walters from Brummer, 1925

Selected References: Hans G. Güterbock, "The Hittite Seals in the Walters Art Gallery" (Essays in Honor of Dorothy Kent Hill), *Journal of The Walters Art Gallery* 36, (1977):11–16; Dorothy Kent Hill, "The Rediscovered Seal of Tarqumuwa, King of Mera," *Archiv Orientalni* 9 (1937):307–10; Jim Hicks et al., *The Empire Builders*, The Emergence of Man, (New York, 1974), 54–55.

— J. V. C.

126 BOUNDARY STONE
Mesopotamian (Cassite period), c.1100 B.C.
Black stone
Height: 11 ½ inches
The Walters Art Gallery (21.10)

125

126

124

127

On one side of this damaged stela is the figure of the king of Babylonia, Marduk-nadin-ahhe. On the top of the other side are symbols of the gods who were to protect the monument. Below these symbols is an inscription that details a royal grant of tax exemption. The piece was excavated by the German expedition to Babylon during the early part of this century.

Provenance: Babylon, debris of a Parthian building

Selected References: R. Koldewey, *Die Tempel von Babylon und Borsippa,* Wissenshaftliche Veröffentlichung der Deutschen Orient-Gesellschaft, (Leipzig, 1911), 46, fig.73; J. V. Canby, *The Ancient Near East in the Walters Art Gallery* (Baltimore, 1974), no.11.

——————————————————————*J.V.C.*

127 STATUETTE
Egyptian (Persian period), c.450 B.C.
Greenish stone
Height: 10 ⅞ inches
The Walters Art Gallery (22.208)

This Egyptian work is unusual in that it represents a man dressed in a long Persian cloak, who crosses his hands in a contemplative and completely un-Egyptian fashion. It is an extremely important and rare example of foreign influence encroaching on age-old Egyptian images during a period of foreign domination.

Provenance: Purchased by Henry Walters from Dikran Kelekian, 1925

Selected Reference: George Steindorff, *Catalogue of the Egyptian Sculpture in The Walters Art Gallery* (Baltimore, 1946), no.149, pl.25.

——————————————————————*J.V.C.*

128 VASE
Greek, Attic red-figure lekythos ("Kertch" style, 360–350 B.C.)
Terra-cotta
Height: 14 inches; Diameter: 4 ⅛ inches
The Walters Art Gallery (48.84)

The main scene shows a game of knucklebones played by a satyr and a nymph. The nymph has caught three knucklebones on the back of her right hand, while the less-skilled satyr has caught only one. The game is observed by Aphrodite, goddess of love and marriage, who is attended by Erotes (small, winged gods of love) and by a youth (perhaps the herdsman Daphnis, intended groom of the nymph). To the right are a female figure, perhaps Peitho, goddess of Persuasion, and a nymph and youth.

The delicate drawing and close attention to detail in the figural scene and ornamental borders enhance the elegant shape of the vase, well adapted to its function as container and dispenser of olive oil. The complex ornament and crowded composition, with its lavish use of added white and other colors, including raised gilded areas such as the bunches of grapes, are typical of vase painting in Athens during the fourth century B.C.

The vase was found at Apollonia, in Thrace (northern Greece) and was purchased by Henry Walters in 1906 at the sale of the Van Branteghem collection.

Selected References: Walters Art Gallery, *Handbook of the Collection* (Baltimore, 1936), 34; Henri Metzger, *Les représenta-*

tions dans la céramique attique du IVᵉ siècle, Bibliothèque des Ecoles Françaises, fasc.172, (Paris, 1951), 398.

——————————————————————*D.M.B.*

129 STATUETTE (ISIS-APHRODITE)
Egyptian or Syrian, 3d century B.C.
Bronze
Height: 18 inches
The Walters Art Gallery (54.949)

This syncretic goddess of fertility and love may have been part of the household shrine of a well-to-do matron of the Roman Empire. She wears a double *stephane* (diadem), earrings, armlets, and a pendant necklace with the central crescent symbolizing Isis, Egyptian goddess of fertility and childbirth. The extended right hand would have held an attribute.

Analogous figurines suggest that the absent right arm was held in an attitude similar to the left arm's. This pose may be a reference to the Hellenistic Anadyomene type, in which Aphrodite shakes the foam from her hair after having risen from the sea. The rounded chin and cheeks, heavy features, and thick, clearly differentiated

128

129

strands of hair recall sculpture of the Severan period (A.D. 193–235). Similar heads can be observed on the Victories and Cupids sarcophagus (A.D. 210), also collected by Henry Walters and now on permanent exhibition in The Walters Art Gallery (23.36).

Provenance: Purchased in 1913 from the Borelli Bey collection of antiquities

Selected References: Margarete Bieber, *Die Antiken Skulpturen und Bronzen des Konigl. Museum Fridericianum in Cassel* (Marburg, 1915), 60; Dorothy K. Hill, *Catalogue of Classical Bronze Sculpture in The Walters Art Gallery* (Baltimore, 1949), no. 206, pl. 43; Ellen Reeder Williams, "A Bronze Statuette of Isis-Aphrodite," *Journal of the American Research Center in Egypt,* 16 (1979): 93–99.

———————————————— *G. A.*

130 DANCING NIKE, formerly with wings
From Myrina, 2d century B.C.
Terra-cotta
Height: 10 ½ inches
The Walters Art Gallery (48.295)

130

This remarkable figurine, preoccupied with dancing in air, was discovered by French archaeologists during their excavations of the necropolis of Myrina between 1880 and 1882. Henry Walters purchased the piece from the art dealer Joseph Brummer in 1925. The figurine was mold-made, and therefore mass-produced, in the workshop of a nameless coroplast. The head, wings (which once fit into slots on her back), right leg, and feet were individually cast. Similar figurines are in the collections of the Louvre, of The Museum of Fine Arts, Boston, and of The J. Paul Getty Museum, Malibu; but of all her "sisters," the Walters figurine exhibits the most stunning combination of gesture and expression, and is considered a masterpiece.

Selected References: Dorothy K. Hill, *The Dance in Classical Times* (Baltimore, 1945), 12; Lillian B. Lawler, *Dance in Ancient Greece* (London, 1964), 103, fig. 39; Lawler, "The Story of the Dance in Ancient Times," *Dance Perspectives,* 13 (1962): 44.

———————————————— *G. A.*

131 HORSE'S HEAD AND SWORD
Roman, A.D. 1st century
Gilded bronze
Length (horse's head): 21 ½ inches; Length (sword): 28 inches
The Walters Art Gallery (54.759)

13

These powerful fragments of a horse's head and a sword were purchased in 1902. The fabric and size of the sword suggest that the two pieces were part of the same group—a Roman Imperial monument or a chariot group.

Provenance: Found in 1884 at Susa, near Ancona, Italy; Massarenti Collection

Selected References: Dorothy K. Hill, *Catalogue of Classical Bronze Sculpture in the Walters Art Gallery* (Baltimore, 1949) 6–7, nn. 10, 10a, pl. 45; Horse's head: H. v. Roques de Maumont *Antike Reiterstandbilden* (Berlin, 1958), 85, fig. 44.

———————————————— *G. A.*

132 PORTRAIT HEAD OF AUGUSTUS
Roman, before A.D. 14
Marble
Height: 15 ⅞ inches
The Walters Art Gallery (23.21)

This portrait of Augustus is one of the few made of the emperor during his lifetime. The subtly modulated planes create the impression of a tense, alert, physically alive presence and facilitate the delicate play of light and shadow over the entire physiognomy. The straight cutting at the top and side of the head indicate a change of material—perhaps to a cheaper marble—for the toga, which was once drawn over the subject's head.

Provenance: Purchased by Henry Walters from Dikran Kelekia in 1913

Selected References: Günter Grimm, *Römische Mummienmasken aus Aegypten* (Wiesbaden, 1974), 110; Walters Art Gallery, *Handbook of the Collection* (Baltimore, 1936), 39; Paul Zanker, *Studien zu den Augustus-Porträts, I: Der Actium Typus* (Göttingen, 1973), 44, fig. 34a.

———————————————————————— G. A.

133   PLATE

Roman (found near Jerusalem), 1st century B.C. to A.D. 1st century
Molded glass
Diameter: 6 ⅜ inches
The Walters Art Gallery (47.75)

The term *millefiori* (after the Italian for "a thousand flowers") is often used to describe the mosaic glass technique that was used to produce this plate. Bundles of monochrome glass rods were heat-fused, cooled, and then cut crosswise to the desired length. The pieces were placed into an outer mold, with an inner mold fitted into the concavity to hold them together. Slow heating in a furnace caused the pieces to fuse but not to become so hot and soft that the pattern was lost. After cooling, the object was removed from its mold and ground and polished on a lathe or with abrasives.

The golden patina on this plate—a quality which is highly prized by collectors—is the result of weathering, or devitrification, caused by the chemical interaction of the surface of the glass with its environment.

Provenance: Purchased by Henry Walters from Dikran Kelekian in 1912

Selected Reference: *3000 Years in Glass*, The Walters Art Gallery, exh. cat. (Baltimore, 1982), no.12.

———————————————————————— G. A.

134   MENOLOGION FOR JANUARY

Constantinople, mid-11th century
11 ¾ x 9 ½ inches
The Walters Art Gallery (MS.W. 521, De Ricci 16)

With regard to uniqueness, a Menologion (calendar of saints and feasts) for the month of January is the single most important codex among the score of Byzantine illuminated examples acquired by Henry Walters. The text, to which is appended Saint John Chrysostom's eulogy on Meletius, archbishop of Antioch (celebrated on 12 February), is the only one of its kind preserved. Containing twenty-one biographies of saints venerated during January in a sequence observed in the redaction of the imperial Menologion, the volume also includes three homilies on the baptism of

Christ, the preaching of Saint John the Baptist, and the veneration of the chains of Peter (6, 7, and 16 January).

Each day's text opens with a generously scaled miniature spanning both well-written columns below. Within the allotted space, the figures are depicted against resplendent gold grounds in active poses (most often in scenes of martyrdom). Others are centered frontally, blessing, occasionally as orants, often holding a book. Landscape and architectural elements enliven all twenty-four richly colored miniatures in this incomplete series for the thirty-one-day month. Of note among the structural backdrops are reminiscences of Roman stage sets and a three-domed church, for which identification with the now-destroyed Church of the Holy Apostles, Constantinople, has been proposed.

An acrostic at the end of each text, spelling out "MICHAEL P" or "MICHAEL P K," has given rise to scholarly debate. According to recent opinion, Michael the Patriarch Keroularios (1043–58) may have been the patron for whom the Menologion was illuminated by a master and assistants, representing top caliber workmanship within the Constantinopolitan tradition.

Provenance: At one time in Armenian hands, as indicated by quire numbers listed on folio 1: Greek Patriarchal Library of

Alexandria, cod. 33, until shortly before 1914: acquired from firm of Gruel, Paris

Selected References: *Illuminated Greek Manuscripts from American Collections. An Exhibition in Honor of Kurt Weitzmann*, ed. Gary Vikan, Princeton University Art Museum (Princeton, 1973), no.11; Iohannis Spatharakis, *Corpus of Dated Illuminated Greek Manuscripts to the Year 1453* (Leiden, 1982), I, no.306.

———————————————————————— L. M. C. R.

135   THE FOUR GOSPELS

Armenian (Cilicia), A.D. 1262
12 x 8 ½ inches
The Walters Art Gallery (MS.W. 539)

According to an account preserved in the museum's files, Henry Walters bought this masterpece of Armenian illumination from the dealer Dikran Kelekian in Paris "one Saturday morning in 1929. He took it with him to the Ritz where he spent the whole afternoon looking at it."

The Gospelbook that so intrigued the eighty-one-year-old Mr. Walters is the most extensively illustrated work by the scribe-

133

132

134

artist T'oros Roslin that has been preserved. This master craftsman, one of the great illuminators of all time, was the head of an extremely active scriptorium in the patriarchal see of Hromkla, Cilicia, during the middle decades of the thirteenth century. The Walters codex, one of seven known in which his name is recorded, contains a dazzling wealth of ornamentation in its Canon Tables, fifteen full-page miniatures, and sixty-seven New Testament representations of various sizes distributed around the text throughout the 410-folio volume.

Artistically, this pictorial compendium, completed with one or more assistants, marks the culmination in T'oros Roslin's oeuvre of the successful fusion of Armenian, Byzantine, and western characteristics into a magnificent symphony of colors and forms. "I, according to my ability and with God's help," wrote T'oros in reference to his patron at the end of the Gospel of Saint John, "executed his command, adorning it inside with pure gold and many colors, and on the outside with precious stone." The present binding, ornamented with glittering stones around a silver-gilt cross, was applied in the second quarter of the seventeenth century.

The fame of the codex was such that it inspired illuminators who had access to the manuscript in its seventeenth-century location in Sebastia, to model certain compositions in their newly created Gospelbooks on designs created by T'oros Roslin some four centuries earlier.

Provenance: Commissioned by the priest T'oros, nephew of the catholicos Constantine I, at Hromkla, A.D. 1262; presented by T'oros to the hermitage of Ark'aghin, Cilicia, A.D. 1266; Sebastia, Church of the Holy Virgin and Church of the Holy Cross, 17th century to A.D. 1915; acquired from Dikran Kelekian, Paris, 1929

Selected References: Sirarpie Der Nesessian, *Armenian Manuscripts in the Walters Art Gallery* (Baltimore, 1973), 10–30; Sirarpie Der Nersessian, *Armenian Art* (London, 1978), 134–35; Anton von Euw and Joachim Plotzek, *Die Handschriften der Sammlung Ludwig* 1 (Cologne, 1979), 132; Diane Cabelli, Thomas F. Mathews, "The Palette of Khatchatur of Khizan," *The Journal of The Walters Art Gallery* 40 (1982): 38.

— L.M.C.R.

136　BIBLE
South Italian, c.1260–68
14 ½ x 9 ¾ inches
The Walters Art Gallery (MS.W. 152, DeRicci 144)

Among the treasures in the Walters manuscript collection is a sumptuously illuminated Bible long associated with Conradin (d.1268), king of Jerusalem and Sicily, grandson of Frederick II. Disassembled and rebound in the nineteenth century, the codex in its curtailed 164-folio format was acquired by Henry Walters in the early years of this century from the Florentine bookseller, Leo S. Olschki. Of the more than two hundred illuminations in this major portion of the splendid Bible, the most important group artistically consists of fifty-two text illustrations in the wide lower and outer margins. The dynamic sense conveyed by the figures is heightened by imaginative combinations of vibrant tones of blue, red, green, and saffron yellow, which dominate the palette. Set against curiously scalloped-edged backgrounds studded with brightly burnished gold discs, the figures were rendered with expert craftsmanship by a master and several assistants. Byzantine and French artistic influences characterize this outstanding representative among a group of about half-a-dozen extant manuscripts produced by the same South Italian workshop during the latter half of the thirteenth century.

Scholarly interest in the Walters Bible has been given impetus in recent years by the surfacing of several groups of illuminated fragments cut out of pages removed from the manuscript, presumably during the last century. Five large figural representations of the type found in the lower margins were acquired by The Walters Art Gallery in 1953; another lot of thirty miscellaneous excised initials and ornamental fragments, sold in London at Sotheby's in 1981, is currently owned by several dealers. The position of the latter in the "mother-codex" has been painstakingly reconstructed in an article in *The Journal of The Walters Art Gallery* (1982) by Rebecca Corrie, whose Harvard University dissertation under the direction of Ernst Kitzinger

135

136

forms the most complete study to date of the complex questions raised by the illustrative content of the so-called Conradin Bible.

Provenance: Comte Auguste Bastard d'Estang, early 19th century; Fréderic Spitzer, Paris, sale, 1893, no.3030; Charles Stein, Paris; Jacques Rosenthal, Munich, catalogues of 1902 and 1905; Leo S. Olschki, Florence; acquired by Henry Walters, c.1905

Selected References: Dorothy Miner, "Since De Ricci II," *The Journal of The Walters Art Gallery* 21–22, (1968–69):87–92; *Die Zeit der Staufer*, exh. cat., Württembergisches Landesmuseum (Stuttgart, 1977), 1, no.829; Rebecca Corrie, "The Conradin Bible: Since 'Since De Ricci,'" *The Journal of The Walters Art Gallery* 40, (1982):13–24.

137

———————————————— *L.M.C.R.*

138

137   KORAN
Persian, first half of the 15th century
15 ½ x 12 ½ inches
The Walters Art Gallery (MS.W. 563)

Impressive for the beauty of its script, decoration, and original binding, this large Koran of the Timurid period exemplifies the qualities most sought after by Henry Walters in the formation of his manuscript collection. The manuscript is an outstanding representative among the nearly 200 Near Eastern illuminated items that complemented some 550 European codices and leaves acquired within Walters' lifetime.

Written on fine, cream-colored paper in large black *thulth* script enhanced by gold, red, and blue characters, the text of this Koran was enriched by a Persian interlinear gloss and marginal commentaries in gold, blue, red, and black *thulth*. Gold was used consistently for the name of Allah, as well as for inter-sectional ornament and opening lines at major divisions.

Most striking of all from a decorative point of view are fifteen full-size ornamental pages at the beginning and at three subsequent portions of the text. In these designs the incredible skills of calligrapher and illuminator reach a zenith of truly resplendent proportions. According to notes made by Dr. Richard Ettinghausen in the course of his examination of the codex,

> The character of the illuminations . . . shows that this manuscript is still under the influence of the sumptuous, large-sized Korans of the Mongol ruler Uljaitu . . . On the other hand, the more baroque form of the marginal *ansae* and the predominant use of naturalistically conceived floral patterns points to the Timurid period. . . .

The pale-brown morocco, contemporary binding tooled in blind and gold with ornate flap and doublures is a rarity of its kind, and is further notable for its fine state of preservation.

Provenance: Purchased by the dealer Dikran Kelekian in Constantinople; acquired from Kelekian

Selected Reference: Dorothy Miner, *The History of Bookbinding. 525–1950 A.D.*, exh. cat., Baltimore Museum of Art (Baltimore,1957), no.76.

———————————————— *L.M.C.R.*

138   BOOK OF HOURS
Northern French (Tournai?), c.1430–35
8 x 5 ½ inches
The Walters Art Gallery (MS.W. 281, De Ricci 261)

139

Northern European illuminated codices for liturgical and private devotional use form a majority among the 750 manuscripts acquired by Henry Walters between the mid-1890s and 1931, the year of his death. While his penchant for deluxe Books of Hours reflects the taste of his day, more specific motivations can be established for certain of Walters' purchases. Such is the case with this single representative of the more than three hundred French and Belgian manuscripts in the Walters collection.

This prayerbook for private devotion is noteworthy for both historical and artistic reasons. Its twenty-seven miniatures, including the earliest known representation of the Evangelist Luke painting a portrait of the Virgin and Child, are of exceeding aesthetic interest and humane appeal. Realistic details abound, ranging from a thin layer of snow on the stable roof in the Nativity miniature, to a large-scale rendering of the original owner kneeling before his patron saint, Bartholomew.

Illuminated by several artists who were influenced by developments in the Paris workshop headed by the Bedford Master, the pictorial program was carried out with the collaboration of an artist whose hand has been recognized in a slightly earlier Hours in the Morgan Library (MS 453). Inserted coats of arms in the floral borders of the Walters Hours attest to a change of ownership in the early 1430s, when the codex was presented to the bridal couple Thomas de Berlettes and Jeanne de Lannoy, settled near Lille. Visual reference to this union was introduced by the insertion of a full-page miniature showing the Marriage of the Virgin. The connection with the de Lannoy family, ancestors of Henry Walters' brother-in-law Warren Delano, prompted the purchase of this Book of Hours in 1913 from the Paris firm headed by Léon Gruel.

Provenance: Alfred Henry Huth (d.1910); Léon Gruel, Paris; acquired in 1913

Selected References: Dorothy Miner, *Illuminated Books of the Middle Ages and Renaissance*, exh. cat., Baltimore Museum of Art and Walters Art Gallery (Baltimore, 1949), no.99; Lilian Randall, "Henry Walters and the de Lannoy Connection," *The Walters Art Gallery Bulletin* 33, 9 (May 1981); John Plummer, *The Last Flowering. French Painting in Manuscripts 1420–1530*, with the assistance of Gregory Clark, exh. cat., The Pierpont Morgan Library (New York, 1982), no.12.

—————————————————————— *L.M.C.R.*

139 AMĪR KHUSRAW DHILAVĪ, *KHAMSA*
Indian (Lahore), dated (A.D. 1597–98)
11 ¼ x 7 ¾ inches
The Walters Art Gallery (MS.W. 624)

Twenty-one superb miniatures remain in this notable copy of a favorite Persian and Indian classic recast by Amīr Khusraw of Delhi (1253–1325). The illumination was carried out by close to a dozen leading painters associated with the court of the emperor Akbar (r.1556–1605). Some of their names are preserved on the miniatures, while in other instances stylistic attribution rests on signed works in other codices.

The animated figural compositions, set in broadly conceived architectural and landscape settings, combine with ornamented margins in two shades of gold to establish the importance of the Walters *Khamsa* in the history of Mughal painting. An early lacquer binding painted with mythological and hunting scenes in the style of the miniatures contributes to the exceptional artistic interest of the volume.

Its date is known from a scribal colophon on the last folio (211) by one of Akbar's favorite scribes, Muhammad Husayn al-Kashmīrī, whom the emperor honored with the title *Zarīn Qalam* (Golden Pen). The recorded dates, 22 March 1597 to 21 March 1598, document the completion of the text approximately midway through the career of this outstanding calligrapher (d.1611), whose earliest known work is dated 1581.

According to his court historian, Abū'l Fazl, Akbar delighted in having works on ethics, morality, and history, as well as poetic romances, read aloud to him—a service for which a fixed fee per page was paid. An avid patron of the arts, Akbar was instrumental in expanding the scope of painters in his employ by encouraging them to incorporate techniques of modeling and perspective found in European prints and paintings imported for this purpose.

Provenance: Seals on first and last folios bearing names of Muhammad Zākī and Muhammad Shāfī

Selected References: Jeremiah P. Losty, *The Art of the Book in India*, exh. cat., The British Library (London, 1982), no.66; Rekha Morris, "Some Additions to the Known Corpus of Paintings by the Mughal Artist Farrukh Chela," *Ars Orientalis* 13, (1982):135, 140.

—————————————————————— *L.M.C.R.*

140

141

142

140 SILVER DISH
Persian (Sasanian), A.D. 5th–7th century
Silver
Diameter: 9 ⅛ inches; Height: 2 ¹/₁₆ inches
The Walters Art Gallery (57.709)

The scene engraved in low relief shows a king presenting jewelry to his consort. The style is characteristic of the Sasanian period (A.D.226–641), the last great epoch in which native Persian traditions flourished prior to the onslaught of Islam. Such Sasanian works represent another area in which Henry Walters was a pioneer American collector.

Royal works such as this one are usually dated according to the design of the king's crown, which differed with each Sasanian ruler. On this basis, archaeologists have attributed this plate to the reign of Yazdigird II (438–457) or Balash (484–89). Details of style and iconography have caused other scholars to suggest a date in the seventh century.

Selected References: A. U. Pope, *A Survey of Persian Art*, 6 vols. (London, 1939), 1:730f., 4:pl.230A; R. Ghirshman, "Scènes de Banquet sur l'Argenterie Sassanide," *Artibus Asiae* 16, (1953):63ff.; University of Michigan Museum of Art, *Sasanian Silver*, exh. cat. (Ann Arbor, 1967), 101.

—————————————————————— *B.B.*

141 CYLINDRICAL BOX WITH CLASSICAL SCENES
Egyptian ("Hellenistic"), early 6th century
Ivory
Height: 3 5/16 inches; Diameter: 3 1/2 inches
The Walters Art Gallery (71.64)

Carved in bas-relief is an abbreviated depiction of the banquet of the gods, who sit around a tripod table on which the apple of the Hesperides rests. The story is continued around the cylindrical box with Hermes shown awarding the apple to the nude Aphrodite, who stands with Hera and Athena. (For the sources of the story, see A. R. Rose, *Handbook of Greek Mythology,* 6th ed. ⟨London, 1958⟩, 106–07, n.17).

Provenance: Count Girolamo Possenti, Fabriano (his sale, Florence, 29 March 1880, lot 16); Eugene Félix, Cologne (his sale, Cologne, 25 October 1886, lot 319); acquired by Henry Walters in 1926

Selected Reference: W. Volbach, *Elfenbeinarbeiten der Spätantik.* 3d ed. (Mainz, 1976), no.104.

——————————————— *B.B.*

142 OLIPHANT
South Italian, 11th century
Ivory
Length: 17 9/16 inches; Diameter: 4 3/4 inches
The Walters Art Gallery (71.234)

This piece is one of a large group of ivory hunting or signal horns carved by Islamic craftsmen in southern Italy. The vine scroll, with its intertwined animal decoration, is reminiscent of Classical prototypes and Coptic textiles.

Provenance: According to the dealer Heilbronner, Berlin, the horn was purchased from the widow of a general who purportedly received it from the duke of Brunswick: a note in the horn says it was part of the treasures of the house of Brunswick-Lüneburg, known as the Guelph Treasure: acquired in 1926 by Henry Walters from Henri Daguerre, Paris.

Selected References: E. Kühnel, *Die islamischen Elfenbeinskulpturen. 8–13. Jahrhundert* (Berlin, 1971), no.59; R. Randall, Jr., et. al., *Ivories in the Collection of The Walters Art Gallery,* no.247 (forthcoming).

——————————————— *B.B.*

143 CASKET
Byzantine, mid-11th century
Bone
Height: 5 inches; Width: 7 5/16 inches
The Walters Art Gallery (71.298)

This casket belongs to a group of more than forty extant ivory caskets having figurative plaques framed by borders of rosettes in interlocking circles. In the Walters example, the figurative plaques feature putti in the guise of warriors, philosophers, and Dionysiac revelers. The type first appeared during the Macedonian Renaissance of the tenth century; the finest example, the Veroli Casket in the Victoria and Albert Museum, London, dates from the early eleventh century. The Walters casket was probably produced in a related workshop at a slightly later date.

Provenance: Edward Joseph (Sale, Christie's, London, 6 May 1890, lot 1003, and February, 1894, lot 357); Isaac Falcke (Sale, Christie's, London, 19 April 1910, lot 166); purchased by Henry Walters from Jacques Seligmann, Paris, 1910

Selected References: A. Goldschmidt and K. Weitzman, *Die byzantinischen Elfenbeinskulpturen des X.–XIII. Jahrhunderts,* 2 vols. (Berlin, 1930–34), 28–29, no.40; R. Randall, Jr., et al., *Ivories in the Collection of The Walters Art Gallery,* no.200 (forthcoming).

——————————————— *B.B.*

144 JACOB BLESSING MANESSEH AND EPHRAIM
Mosan (workshop of Godefroid de Clair ?),
mid-12th century
Champlevé enamel on gilt copper
Height: 2 7/8 inches; Width: 3 7/8 inches
The Walters Art Gallery (44.97)

This plaque originally formed the top of a large altar cross. According to Genesis 48: 8–20, Jacob crossed his arms to bless his youngest grandchild, Ephraim, with his right hand, while blessing the elder grandchild, Manesseh, with his left. During the Middle Ages, this incident was interpreted analogically as signifying the substitution of the New for the Old Covenant. Later, the gesture also received a typological interpretation as a prefiguration of the Crucifixion.

Selected References: M. C. Ross, "A Mosan Enamel in the Walters Art Gallery," *Revue Belge d'Archéologie et d'Histoire de l'Art* 8, 3 (July–September 1938), 193–95; W. Stechow, "Jacob Blessing the Sons of Joseph," *Gazette des Beaux-Arts* 23, (January–June 1943), 192–208.

——————————————— *B.B.*

145 PERSONIFICATION OF PRUDENCE
North Italian (Verona?), 1170–80
Bronze, cast and chiseled
Height: 4 7/16 inches
The Walters Art Gallery (54.52)

Along with Temperance, Fortitude, and Justice, Prudence was one of the four Cardinal Virtues and was frequently represented in

143

144

145

the guise of an angel during the twelfth century. Based upon the prescription of Saint Matthew (10.16), "Be ye therefore wise as serpents . . . ," the serpent became one of the traditional attributes of Prudence. The Veronese origin has been suggested on the basis of stylistic similarities to the early portions of the doors of San Zeno in that city (A. Broekler, *Die Bronzetur von San Zeno,* Marburg, 1931).

Selected Reference: Metropolitan Museum of Art, *The Year 1200,* K. Hoffman, ed., 2 vols. (New York, 1970), no.129.

——————————————— *B.B.*

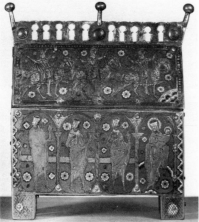

146

148

Provenance: Peytel (?): purchased by Henry Walters from Henri Daguerre, 1927

Selected Reference: The Metropolitan Museum of Art, *The Year 1200*, K. Hoffman, ed., 2 vols. (New York, 1970), 1, no.163.

——————————————— *B.B.*

147   CROZIER

French (Limoges), 1230–50 (?)
Copper gilt and champlevé enamel
Height: 13 inches
The Walters Art Gallery (44.121)

Rows of glass-paste cabochons alternate with four descending lizard-like dragons on the shaft, which is engraved with floral motifs. The knop features three heraldic shields (two bars, azure), alternating with three more shields (three palets, gules), on which the colors are enameled. Two rows of cabochons ornament the upper end of the shaft, which tapers into a volute with a serpent's-head terminal. The Annunciation is represented within the volute.

Provenance: Rev. Walter Sneyd, Keele Hall, Staffordshire (Sale, Christie's, London, July, 1902, no.86); acquired by Henry Walters from Jacques Seligmann, Paris, before 1931

Selected Exhibition: South Kensington Museum, *Catalogue of the Special Exhibition of Works of Art* (1862), London, 1863, no.1098

147

146   CHÂSSE

French (Limoges), 1220–30
Copper, champlevé enamel
Height: 8 ¹¹⁄₁₆ inches; Width: 3 ⅛ inches;
        Length: 7 ¼ inches
The Walters Art Gallery (44.288)

On the upper front plaque, the three Magi are shown riding. In the lower front plaque they stand, each in a columned arch, to present their gifts to the Child, who is held by the Virgin. She sits under a fourth columned arch, enthroned on a rainbow. On each gabled end plaque is a saint, probably an apostle, standing in a mandorla that interrupts a rainbow. The rear panels are decorated with geometric designs.

Selected Reference: J. J. Marquet de Vasselot, *Les Crosses Limousines du XIII⁰ Siècle* (Paris, 1941), 169–70, 250 (no.92), pls.15, 35.

——————————————— *B.B.*

148   CANDLESTICK

Mosan (Dinant ?), 13th century
Bronze, cast and engraved
Height: 15 ¾ inches; Width: 8 ⁵⁄₁₆ inches
The Walters Art Gallery (54.784)

The representation of the man on the lion may refer to the biblical story of Samson and the lion (Judges 14:5–6), a popular medieval theme frequently used for candlesticks (and other objects) serving both liturgical and domestic functions. Like other examples of *dinanderie* inspired by Near Eastern prototypes, the motif of a rider astride a lion may be derived from Islamic astrological images representing the sun in the house of Leo.

Provenance: Baron Albert von Oppenheim, Cologne; J. P. Morgan, Sr.; acquired by Henry Walters in 1923 from A. Seligmann, Rey and Co., New York

Selected References: O. von Falke and E. Meyer, *Romanische Leuchter und Gefässe der Gotik*, (Berlin, 1935), 36, fig.226; Walters Art Gallery, *Liturgical Objects* (Baltimore, 1976), fig.2; G. Swarzenski, "Samson Killing the Lion, A Medieval Bronze Group," *Bulletin of The Museum of Fine Arts [Boston]* 38, 229 (October, 1940), 67–74.

——————————————— *B.B.*

149   CASKET

French (Paris), 1330–50
Ivory
Height: 4 ½ inches; Length: 9 ¹¹⁄₁₆ inches;
        Diameter: 4 ¹³⁄₁₆ inches
The Walters Art Gallery (71.264)

The carvings depict episodes from medieval romances. From left to right on the lid appear the Attack on the Castle of Love, a jousting scene, and a mock tournament between ladies and knights. Aristotle teaching Alexander and its sequel, Phyllis riding Aristotle, occupy the front panel, together with two scenes from the Fountain of Youth. Four scenes are carved on the rear panel: Gawain fighting the lion, Lancelot crossing the sword bridge, Gawain on the perilous bed, and the three maidens at the Chateau Merveil. On the right end-panel, Galahad receives the keys to the Castle of Maidens. Tristam and Iseult with King Mark in the tree and the story of the virgin and the unicorn are carved on the left end-panel. Stylistically, the carving is typical of Parisian work in the second quarter of the fourteenth century. The iron mounts were added during the nineteenth century.

150

149

Provenance: Rev. John Bowle, Wiltshire (c.1780); Gustavus Brander, Christchurch, Hampshire, 1787; Francis Douce, London (until 1824); Sir Samuel Rush Meyrick, Goodrich Court, Herefordshire (until 1848); Lt. Col. Augustus Meyrick; Frederick Spitzer, Paris, (acquired 1871; sold 1896); Oscar Hainauer, Berlin, 1897; Duveen and Co.; H. Economos, London, 1913; purchased by Henry Walters from Arnold Seligmann, Rey & Cie., Paris, 1923

Selected References: John Carter, *Specimens of Ancient Sculpture* (London, 1780), 2:49; R. Koechlin, "Quelques ivoires gothiques français connus antérieurement au XIXᵉ siècle," *La revue de l'art chrétien* 54(1911):396–99; R. S. Loomis, *Arthurian Legends in Medieval Art* (New York, 1938), 66, 70–71, 76; R. Randall, Jr., et al., *Ivories in the Collection of The Walters Art Gallery*, no.324 (forthcoming).

──────────────── *B.B.*

150 MIRROR CASE

North Italian (Milan ?), c.1410
Ivory
Diameter: 3 ³⁄₁₆ inches
The Walters Art Gallery (71.107)

The mirror cover shows a young man offering a flower to a lady. The lovers stand in a garden and both wear elaborate costumes. Inscribed in the banderole above the man's head is the word *prenez* ("take"). The motto is completed with the words *en gré* inscribed on the pendant mirror case, now in the Musée de Cluny, Paris (R. Koechlin, *Les ivoires gothiques français*, Paris, 1924, no.105). Translated as "Take kindly," the motto was used in France and Burgundy, appearing on a goblet in the 1369 inventory of Louis I of Anjou. The full phrase, *Prenez en gré le don de votre amant* ("Take kindly the gift of your lover"), served as the refrain for one of Christine de Pizan's (1364–c.1430) *Cent Balades (Oeuvres Poétiques*, M. Roy ed., 3 vols. ⟨Paris, 1886⟩, 1:81).

Provenance: Pietro di Giacomo Grandenigo, Venice; acquired by Henry Walters in 1914

Selected References: M. Ross, "A Gothic Ivory Mirror Case," *Journal of The Walters Art Gallery* 2, (1939):109–11; R. Randall,

Jr., et al., *Ivories in the Collection of The Walters Art Gallery*, no.348 (forthcoming).

──────────────── *B.B.*

151 PECTORAL CROSS AND CASE

Byzantine, second half of the 16th century
Gold, pearls, rubies, emeralds, amethyst, and pastes
Case cover: 2 ⁹⁄₁₆ x 2 ⁷⁄₁₆ inches;
    Case base: 3 ⅛ x 2 ¹³⁄₁₆ inches;
    Crucifix: 2 ¹⁄₁₆ x 1 ⁵⁄₁₆ inches
The Walters Art Gallery (57.1511 A, B, C)

Although this pendant is one of the most magnificent surviving pieces of sixteenth-century Byzantine jewelry, nothing is known about its immediate provenance other than the fact that it was included in Henry Walters' original bequest.

The pendant consists of two parts, a small pectoral cross and its case. The exterior front cover of the case is decorated with a cameo of the Madonna and Child, surrounded with baroque pearls alternating with jewels and semiprecious stones set onto gold filigree. The rim of the case back is studded with baroque pearls, and its back is decorated with a variety of stones and colored pastes set on a gold filigree background. Encircling the inside face of the

case back is an inscription in niello identifying the original owner: "Arsenius, the most holy metropolitan of Serres and Rypertimos [and] substituting for [the metropolitan of] Caesaria-Capadocia, God be helper." During the middle of the sixteenth century, Arsenius served as metropolitan of Serres (modern Serrai), an important sixteenth- and seventeenth-century artistic center in northeastern Greece (Macedonia), where this pendant may have been made. A later inscription on the crucifix indicates that Arsenius left the pendant "to the monastery of the Holy Trinity called Esoptron on the island of Chalke [Chalkis]."

Selected References: M. C. Ross and B. Laourda, "The Pendant Jewel of the Metropolitan Arsenius," *Beiträge für Georg Swarzenski* (Berlin, 1951), 181–84; Walters Art Gallery, *Jewelry: Ancient to Modern* (New York, 1979), 161, no.460.

──────────────── *B.B.*

GIOVANNI DI PAOLO
Italian (Siena), c.1403–82
152 *The Entombment* (1426)
Oil on panel
15 ⅞ x 17 ¼ inches
The Walters Art Gallery (37.489 D)

Synthesizing a variety of influences into a unique stylistic amalgam, Giovanni's re-

151

152

tivity. The identity of the donor remains unknown, although traces of a necklace uncovered during the 1939 cleaning suggest that he may have been a member of the Order of the Golden Fleece.

Provenance: P. A. Borger, Arnhem (sale, Fr. Muller et Cie., Amsterdam, 13 November 1882, no.16); M. Leembruggen (lent by him to the Rijksmuseum, Amsterdam, 1903–20); Sale, Muller et Cie., 13 April 1920, no.66; New York, private collection; acquired by Henry Walters from Jacques Seligmann, 7 December 1920

Selected References: J. Destrée, *Hugo van der Goes* (Brussels, 1914), 122; Max Friedländer, *Early Netherlandish Painting*, trans. H. Norden (Leyden and Brussels, 1967), 4:30, 71, no.18; Charles de Tolnay, "Hugo van der Goes as Portrait Painter," *Art Quarterly* 8, (1954):181–90; Friedrich Winkler, *Das Werk des Hugo van der Goes* (Berlin, 1964), 86–87; J. Folie, "St. John the Baptist and a Donor," *Flanders in the Fifteenth Century*, exh. cat. (Detroit, 1960), 120–21; R. and M. Wittkower, *Born under Saturn* (New York, 1969, rept. 1974), 108–13.

——————————————————————————— *B.B.*

CARLO CRIVELLI
Italian (Venetian), 1430/35–c.1495
154 *Madonna and Child with Saints* (c.1490)
Oil on panel
38 ⁹⁄₁₆ x 32 ⁵⁄₁₆ inches
The Walters Art Gallery (37.593)

Little is known about Crivelli's life, and he is not mentioned by Vasari. Surviving documents suggest that he launched his career in Venice, that he was resident in Zara in Dalmatia about 1465, and that about 1468 he settled in the Marches, where he worked assiduously until his death. Influenced by the Paduan painter, Francesco Squarcione, and his pupil, Paolo Schiavoni, Crivelli developed a unique style combining orna-

fined technique and elegant draftsmanship made him one of the leading exponents of the "International Style." This work is one of four predella panels acquired by Walters that belong to Giovanni's earliest signed and dated work, the now dispersed polyptych painted for the Pecci-Paganucci chapel in San Domenico, Siena. Giovanni has conflated the Lamentation and the Entombment in a composition that recalls Byzantine prototypes that show Christ being buried in a cave rather than in a sarcophagus, as is more common in the western depictions. The drama suggested by the gestures and expressive physiognomies is enhanced by the remarkable shadow cast by Nicodemus (?), which represents one of the earliest post-Classical attempts to depict this natural phenomenon.

Provenance: Pecci-Paganucci altar, San Domenico, Siena (1426–mid-16th century); Malavolti altar, San Domenico (mid-16th century–mid-17th century); refectory, San Domenico (mid-17th–late 18th century); Comm. Galgano Saracini, Siena (by 1819); Counts Chigi-Saracini, Siena; acquired in 1911 by Henry Walters from Luigi Grassi, Florence.

Selected References: C. Brandi, "Ricostruzione di un'opera giovanile di Giovanni di Paolo," *L'Arte* 37, fasc. 6 (November 1934), 462–81; M. Meiss, "Some Remarkable Early Shadows in a Rare Type of Threnos," *Festschrift Ulrich Middeldorf* (Berlin, 1968), 112–18; F. Zeri, *Italian Paintings in the Walters Art Gallery*, 2 vols. (Baltimore, 1976), 1:118–21.

——————————————————————————— *B.B.*

HUGO VAN DER GOES
Flemish (Ghent), c.1440–82
153 *Donor with Saint John the Baptist*
(after 1477)
Oil on oak panel
12 ¹¹⁄₁₆ x 8 ¾ inches
The Walters Art Gallery (37.296)

Among the most precious objects acquired by Henry Walters is this small panel. Unanimously attributed to Hugo van der Goes, it is one of only about eighteen surviving paintings by this influential master. Sponsored by Joos van Ghent, Hugo received his patent as a master in the painters' guild of his native city in 1467. Enjoying considerable patronage, he was elected dean of the guild in 1474, but abruptly ended his public career the following year, becoming a monk in the *Rode Klooster* (Red Cloister) near Brussels. The chronicle of a fellow monk, Gaspar Ofhuys, indicates that he continued to paint for important patrons, although he suffered from an increasingly severe mental disorder described as *frensis magna* ("great raging of the brain"). His intense melancholy apparently abated shortly prior to his death.

The Walters panel may have been trimmed in length and is perhaps the surviving half of a diptych. On stylistic grounds, it is assigned to the artist's last period of ac-

153

154

man prototypes of the late Middle Ages. Its hieratic quality was enhanced when the panel was cut down—probably at the end of the eighteenth century—removing the head of Saint John, at whom the Madonna gazed. Without this human focus, the Madonna's expression appears abstract and remote, qualities that attracted Ingres, who quoted the figure in several paintings. Henry Walters was a great admirer of medieval art, as well as of Ingres, and shared the French artist's enthusiasm for the painting, although it represented a later phase in the master's style than was generally popular at the turn of the century. Walters' acquisition was the first example of a Raphael Madonna to enter an American collection.

Provenance: Borghese collection, Rome; Lucien Bonapart; Maria Louisa, Queen of Etruria, Lucca; H. A. J. Munro, Novar, Scotland; Henry Alexander Munro Butler Johnston; acquired by Henry Walters in 1901, probably through Ichenhauser, London

Selected References: David Allan Brown, *Raphael and America*, exh. cat., National Gallery of Art (Washington, DC, 1983), 72–79; Federico Zeri, *Italian Paintings in the Walters Art Gallery*, 2 vols. (Baltimore, 1976), 2:348–54.

———————————————————— *B.B.*

GIOVANNI DEI BERNARDI DA CASTELBOLOGNESE
Italian, 1496–1553
156 *Fall of Phaeton* (1533–35)
Rock crystal, engraved in intaglio on reverse
Height: 2 ^{15}/₁₆ inches; Width: 2 ^{7}/₁₆ inches
The Walters Art Gallery (41.69)

Described by Saba da Castiglione as the greatest cutter of gems and dies for coins since antiquity (*Ricordi*, Venice, 1607 fol. 115; Ricordo 109), Giovanni was admired as well by Benvenuto Cellini and Vasari.

Between June and September 1533, Michelangelo sent his friend, Tommaso de'Cavalieri, three drawings representing the *Fall of Phaeton* (Ovid, *Metamorphoses*,

155

mental richness with an emotional expressiveness that depends to a major degree upon the artist's highly refined draftsmanship. His numerous altarpieces are notable for their exquisite coloring and for the plasticity of the figures.
Madonna is flanked by Saint Francis of Assisi on her right and Saint Bernardino of Siena on her left. The diminutive donor kneeling on the parapet wears Franciscan robes, suggesting that the panel was commissioned for a Franciscan church or monastery. The painting was acquired by Henry Walters in 1902, when he purchased the Don Marcello Massarenti collection.

Provenance: Don Marcello Massarenti, purchased by Henry Walters in 1902

Selected References: Pietro Zampetti, *Paintings from the Marches: Gentile to Raphael* (London, 1971), 175–82; Federico Zeri, *Italian Paintings in the Walters Art Gallery*, 2 vols. (Baltimore, 1976), 1:242–43.

———————————————————— *B.B.*

RAPHAEL (RAFFAELLO SANZIO) AND WORKSHOP
Italian, 1483–1520
155 *Madonna of the Candelabra* (1513–14)

Oil on panel
Height: 25 ¼ inches; Width: 25 ⅞ inches (tondo)
The Walters Art Gallery (37.484)

Raphael's reputation as the most perfect painter began before his death and flourished among artists and connoisseurs well into the twentieth century, when American merchant princes sought to crown their new collections of Old Masters by acquiring one of his rare works. A child prodigy, Raphael received his earliest training from his father, Giovanni Santi, but formed his style in the workshop of Pietro Perugino. In Florence from 1504 to 1508, he was profoundly influenced by Leonardo da Vinci and Michelangelo. Summoned to Rome in 1508, he brilliantly synthesized Classical and modern sources, creating paintings and frescoes in which the grace of the figures, harmony of the colors, and balance of the composition epitomize the ideals of the High Renaissance.
The *Madonna of the Candelabra* belongs to the artist's middle Roman period; only the central figures are by the master's hand. The composition is based upon Ro-

156

11.300ff.), which are now in the British Museum, London; the Royal Library, Windsor; and the Accademia delle Belli Arti, Venice (Frey 57, 58, 75). Together with two other drawings, representing *Tityos* and the *Rape of Ganymede,* Michelangelo's gifts to Tommaso were evidently secured by Cardinal Ippolito de'Medici, who commissioned Giovanni to carve the designs on crystal plaquettes. These were to be set in a silver casket, which remained unfinished at the time of Ippolito's death in August 1535.

Although it differs somewhat from the casts and impressions identified by Slomann, the signed Walters crystal presumably originated with this commission. In adopting Michelangelo's design, Giovanni deleted the figure of Zeus entirely and characteristically modified Michelangelo's composition in depicting Phaeton and his horses. The figures of the river god, Eridanus, and of the Heliades being transformed into poplar trees, are derived from the British Museum drawing. From the Windsor drawing come the figure of Cygnus, who was transformed into a swan, and the man carrying an urn, whom Giovanni moved to the extreme left.

157

Inscription: *IOVANES*

Provenance: Strozzi family, sold by Count Max Strozzi to R. Heilbronner, Paris, from whom it was acquired by Henry Walters prior to 1931

Selected References: Vasari, *Vitae,* ed. Milanesi, 5:374; V. Slomann, "Rock Crystals by Giovanni Bernardi," *Burlington Magazine* 48, (1926):9–23; N. Krasnowa, "Rock-Crystals by Giovanni Bernardi in the Hermitage Museum," *Burlington Magazine* 56, (1930):37–38; M. C. Ross, "Six Engraved Rock Crystals in the Walters Art Gallery," *Magazine of Art* 30, 1(January 1937):21–23ff.

———————————————————— *B.B.*

GIOVANNI DEI BERNARDI DA CASTELBOLOGNESE
Italian, 1496–1553
157 *Christ before Pilate* (1539 or 1546/47)
Rock crystal
Height: 2 ¹³⁄₁₆; Length: 3 ½ inches
The Walters Art Gallery (41.240)

Among the projects mentioned by Vasari in his life of Giovanni were two series of rock crystals engraved with scenes from the Passion of Christ, both commissioned by Cardinal Alessandro Farnese. Letters published by Ronchini from the artist to his patron indicate that they were completed in 1539 and 1547. Including the Walters plaque, nineteen crystals that can be associated with the Farnese commissions survive. Thirteen are set in the silver altar cross and pair of candlesticks made by Antonio Gentile da Faenza and presented by the Cardinal to the Basilica of Saint Peter, Rome; four are mounted in a silver casket in the National Museum, Copenhagen; and one has been acquired recently by the National Gallery of Art, Washington, DC. In listing the subjects of the plaques, Vasari writes of one showing Christ "led before Annas, Herod, and Pilate" (*quando e menato ad Anna, Erode e Pilato*), although Giovanni presumably followed the traditional iconographic formula and represented these distinct episodes on separate plaques.

Provenance: Sir Francis Cook; Humphrey W. Cook (sale, Christie's, London, 10 July 1925, lot 469); Henry Walters; Mrs. Henry Walters (sale, Parke-Bernet, New York, 4 December 1943, lot 996)

Selected References: Vasari, *Vitae,* ed. Milanesi, 5:373–74; V. Slomann, "Rock-crystals by Giovanni Bernardi," *Burlington Magazine* 48(1926):9–23; E. Kris, *Meister und Meisterwerke der Steinschneidekunst in der Italienischen Renaissance,* 2 vols. (Vienna, 1929), 69–72; E. Kris, "Di alcune opere ignote di Giovanni dei Bernardi nel Tesoro di San Pietro," *Dedalo* 9(1928):97; A. Ronchini, "Maestro Giovanni di Castel Bolognese," *Atti e Memorie della RR. deputazioni di storia per le provincie Modenesi et Parmensi,* 4(1868):1–28; M. C. Ross, "A Rock-Crystal Carving by Giovanni dei Bernardi da Castelbolognese," *Art Quarterly* 9(1946):80–82.

———————————————————— *B.B.*

158

COULY NOUAILHER
French (Limoges), flourished during the second
     third of the 16th century
158 *Casket: Scenes of the Life of Hercules*
     (mid-16th century)
Enamel on copper
Height: 5 ⅛ inches; Length: 7 ½ inches;
     Width: 4 ¾ inches
The Walters Art Gallery (44.65)

Set within a contemporary, Classical-style, gilt-metal frame are ten plaques depicting incidents in the life of Hercules (Apollodorus, *The Library,* II, iv. 8ff.). On the sloping sides of the trapezoidal lid are shown Hercules and the Nemean Lion, the capture of the Cretan bull, the carrying of the "Pillars of Hercules," and the killing of Cacus (inscribed: *ERCVLE CACCUS*). On the back of the chest are shown the fight with Achelous for Dejanira (inscribed: *ACHELOO ERCVLES*) and the capture of Cerberus (inscribed: *CERBUROCAN ERCVLES*). On the left end of the chest Hercules is shooting with his bow at Nessus, the centaur, who is absconding with Dejanira (inscribed: *ERCVLES DIANIRA*). On the right end of the chest, Theseus is shown fighting Jason, and Hercules is depicted wresting Dejanira from Nessus (inscribed: *TESEO IASON ERCVLES DIANIRA*). On the front of the chest is the fight with the Lernean Hydra (inscribed: *LIDRAN ERCVLES*) and the immolation of Hercules, shown with Poias, who kindled the pyre (inscribed: *COUMAN ERCLVES FINOCYE IOR*). On either end of the lid are trapezoidal plaques showing a female head in three-quarter view, in a medallion surrounded by four cornucopias supported by two standing putti.

The representations of Hercules' life may have been inspired by the reliefs on the rood screen of Limoges cathedral, commissioned by Jean de Langeac, bishop of Limoges, and carved between 1532 and 1541. These scenes are themselves derived from

Italian prototypes (cf. A. Cloulas-Brousseau, "Le Jubé de la Cathédrale de Limoges," *Bulletin de la Société Archéologique et Historique du Limousin* 90, ⟨1963⟩:101–88). A number of related caskets and plaques have been identified by Philippe Verdier.

Provenance: Lord Hastings, sold 1888; acquired by Henry Walters from G. R. Harding, 1919

Selected References: J. B. Waring, *Art Treasures of the United Kingdom from the Art Treasures Exhibition* (Manchester, 1858), no.68; Philippe Verdier, *Catalogue of the Painted Enamels of the Renaissance* (Baltimore, 1977), no.67.

——————————————————————— *B.B.*

ATTRIBUTED TO ANDREA BRIOSCO
(called "IL RICCIO")
Italian (Padua), 1470/75–1532
159   *Seated Shepherd with Syrinx*   (c.1505–20)
Bronze, natural brown patina with remnants of
   black lacquer patina and traces of strong green
   patina
Height: 8 ¾ inches
The Walters Art Gallery (54.234)

A student of Bartolomeo Bellano (c.1440–96/97), Riccio was one of the most popular artists of his day. Associated with the circle of Paduan humanists including Giovanni Battista de Leone and Leonicus, he adapted and transformed antique prototypes, producing many small bronzes evoking the world of Classical paganism, which were highly prized by learned, aristocratic collectors.

Although the subject of this statuette has not been firmly established, Bowron suggests that it represents Daphnis, the son of Hermes, who, having been struck blind when he betrayed the love of a nymph, was taught to play the Syrinx by Pan and became

159

the inventor of pastoral music (Diodorus Siculus, *Bibliotheca Historica,* IV, 84).

First attributed to Riccio by Verdier, the Walters bronze is an *unicum,* a unique cast—related, however, to bronzes in the Louvre, Paris, and the Ashmolean Museum, Oxford. Although he initially accepted this attribution, Sir John Pope-Hennessey (1962, orally) has subsequently suggested Vettor Gambello, called Camelio (c.1455/60–1537), as the author.

Provenance: Jacques Seligmann, Paris; acquired by Henry Walters before 1931

Selected References: Edgar Peters Bowron, *Renaissance Bronzes in the Walters Art Gallery* (Baltimore, 1978), 32–34; Wendy Stedman Sheard, *Antiquity in the Renaissance* (Northampton, 1978), no.110; P. Verdier, "An Unknown Riccio," *Bulletin of the Walters Art Gallery* 6, 6(March 1954):1–3.

——————————————————————— *B.B.*

FRANCESCO XANTO AVELLI DA ROVIGO
(called "FRA XANTO" or "ROVIGO DA URBINO")
Italian, flourished 1528–42
160   *Bottle with Stopper*   (1530)
Majolica, painted in blue, copper-green, yellow,
   ochre, manganese, black, and opaque white
Height: 14 ¹⁵⁄₁₆ inches; Width: 8 ¾ inches
The Walters Art Gallery (48.1373)

Born around 1500, Xanto was active in Urbino during the third and fourth decades of the sixteenth century. He was among the most prolific followers of the finest master of historiated majolica, Nicola Pellipario (c.1480–1547). An author as well as an illustrator, Xanto specialized in scenes representing episodes from Classical history and mythology and from contemporary poetry.

Typically, Xanto adopted figures from various engravings in composing his illustrations. His depiction of *Mercury Conducting Psyche to Olympus* (Apulius, *The Golden Ass,* VI) on the front of this bottle is probably based upon the engraving by Gian Jacopo Caralgio (Bartsch, XV.50), after Raphael's frescoed lunette in the Villa Farnesina, Rome. On the reverse, a muscular nude hurls a wineskin over his head; to his left, a winged cupid struggles to lift another wineskin, over which he has slung his bow. J. C. Robinson described the bottle as "perhaps the finest work of its kind by him [Xanto] now extant" when it was exhibited at the South Kensington Museum (now Victoria and Albert Museum), London, in 1861 (no.5237).

Inscription: (on the neck): *F.A.R.* and *M.D.XXX*

Provenance: Samuel Addington (said to have acquired it in Spain); M. P. W. Boulton (sale, Christie's, London, 15 December

160

1911, no.92); acquired by Henry Walters in 1914 from G. R. Harding

Selected References: J. C. Robinson, ed., *Catalogue of the Special Exhibition of works of Art . . . on Loan at the South Kensington Museum, June 1862,* (London, 1863), 427–28; J. P. von Erdberg, "Early Work by Fra Xanto Avelli da Rovigo in the Walters Art Gallery," *Journal of The Walters Art Gallery* 13–14, (1950–51):31–37; J. P. von Erdberg and M. C. Ross, *Catalogue of the Italian Majolica in the Walters Art Gallery* (Baltimore, 1952), no.51.

——————————————————————— *B.B.*

WORKSHOP OF GUIDO DURANTINO
Italian (Urbino), before 1520–after 1576
161   PLATE   (c.1535)
Majolica, painted in blue, turquoise-blue, copper-
   green, yellow, ochre, brown, tan, gray, black,
   and opaque white
Diameter: 9 ¾ inches
The Walters Art Gallery (48.1368)

The Durantino workshop in Urbino practiced the style of *istoriato* painting perfected by Guido's more gifted father, Nicola Pellipario (c.1480–1547). Decorated with the legend of Apollo and Daphne (Ovid, *Metamorphoses,* Book 1), this plate was produced as part of Durantino's most notable commission, the service made in 1535 for Duke Anne de Montmorency, *grand maitre* (afterwards Constable) of France. Rackham suggests that the illustration may be an autograph work by Durantino.

161

Inscription: (on the reverse): *Apollo Sequita/Daphne qual se/conuerb in Lauro/In botega Guido/durantino in/urbino*

Provenance: Baron Seillière Coll.(?): Thomas B. Clarke (sale, American Art Galleries, New York, 8 January 1916, no.609): acquired by Henry Walters in 1916 from G. R. Harding

Selected References: J. P. von Erdberg and M. C. Ross, *Catalogue of Italian Majolica in the Walters Art Gallery* (Baltimore, 1952), no.46: Bernard Rackham, "The Maiolica-Painter Guido Durantino," *Burlington Magazine* 77 (1940): 182–88.

———————————————————— *B.B.*

GIANLORENZO BERNINI AND WORKSHOP
Italian (Rome), 1598–1680
162 *The Risen Christ* (c.1673–74)
Bronze
Height: 17 5/16 inches (including hand)
The Walters Art Gallery (54.2281), Gift of C. Morgan Marshall, 1942

This bronze statuette was intended to crown the new altarpiece that Bernini designed for the Cappella del SS. Sacramento in the Basilica of Saint Peter, Rome. Originally commissioned by Pope Urban VIII in 1629, the tabernacle was actually constructed between November 1672 and December 1674. To celebrate the Eucharist, Bernini conceived the altarpiece as a monumental ciborium in the shape of a circular temple, surrounded by a ring of columns with gilt-bronze statuettes of the Apostles on their entablature and flanked by two colossal adoring angels. Standing atop the dome and gazing down at his worshipers with his hand

162

163

raised in benediction, the figure of Christ symbolized his triumph over death.

Several assistants were involved in the production of this complex altarpiece. Following Bernini's designs, Giovanni Rinaldi carved a clay model of the *Risen Christ* from which the plaster and wax molds necessary for casting were prepared by other assistants. A flawed cast, the Walters bronze was presumably rejected because of a crack running across the chest. The statue was cast again and it is this version which now surmounts the tabernacle in Rome. Henry Walters kept this bronze in his downtown Baltimore office.

Provenance: Henry Walters: C. Morgan Marshall

Selected References: M. S. Weil, "A Statuette of the Risen Christ Designed by Gian Lorenzo Bernini," *Journal of the Walters Art Gallery* 29–30, (1966–67):7–15: M. P. Mezzatesta, *The Art of Gianlorenzo Bernini*, exh. cat. (Fort Worth, 1982), no.11: C. Snow, "Examination of a Bernini Bronze," *Journal of The Walters Art Gallery* 41, (1983), 77–79.

———————————————————— *B.B.*

163 SNUFFBOX
French, 1750-56
Goldsmith: Philippe Emmanuel Garbe,
  Master 1748–93
Height: 1 3/8 inches; Length: 3 inches;
  Width: 2 1/8 inches
The Walters Art Gallery (57.155)

The rectangular gold box is set with panels of Japanese black and gold lacquer.

Marks: Charge and discharge marks for *sous-fermier* Julien Berthe 1750–56: mark for goldsmith Philippe Emmanuel Garbe, master at Quai Pelletier, Paris, 1748–93

Provenance: James A. Garland: Brayton Ives: E. M. Harding to Henry Walters in 1916

———————————————————— *W.R.J.*

164 WATCH CASE
French, 1754/55
Goldsmith: Jacques de La Feuille, Paris
Diameter: 1 7/8 inches
The Walters Art Gallery (58.44)

The gold case is chiseled and painted in black and gold to simulate Japanese seventeenth-century lacquer. Both the white enamel dial set with diamond brilliants and the English movement engraved "Jno. Russel, London" post-date the case.

Marks: Date-letter for 1754/55: discharge mark of *sous-fermier* Julien Berthe: mark of goldsmith Jacques La Feuille

Provenance: Collection Anatole Demidoff, prince of San Donato, Tiffany and Company, New York, 1893, no.13, to Henry Walters

———————————————————— *W.R.J.*

165 A PAIR OF POTPOURRI VASES
French (Sèvres), c.1762
Soft-paste porcelain, gilt-bronze bases
Height: 12 inches
The Walters Art Gallery (48.590)

These vases feature a *bleu celeste* ground with chinoiserie terrace-scene vignettes inspired by Chinese eighteenth-century enamels or porcelains.

Mr. and Mrs. Henry Walters were particularly drawn to French eighteenth-century decorative arts. In 1928, they purchased the E. M. Hodgkins collection of Sèvres porcelains, which had been formed in the last quarter of the nineteenth century, when such wares became available following political upheavals in France.

Marks: Marks are concealed by the mountings

Provenance: E. M. Hodgkins: E. Chappey: Arnold Seligmann, Rey & Co. to Henry Walters in 1928

———————————————————— *W.R.J.*

164

165

166

EDOUARD MANET
French, 1832–83
167 *At the Café* (1879)
Oil on fabric
18 ^{11}/₁₆ x 15 ^{7}/₁₆ inches
The Walters Art Gallery (37.893)

Although he shared his father's preference for finely executed art, Henry Walters endeavored to enrich the senior Walters' collections with works that would provide a more comprehensive view of the nineteenth century's artistic achievements. In so doing, the younger Walters acquired a number of paintings by the modernists. Manet's café scene showing a couple in the Brasserie de Reichshoffen, Paris, was purchased from the dealer Joseph Durand-Ruel, with whom Henry had attended school in Paris during the American Civil War.

Signed: (at lower left): *Manet*

Provenance: A. M. Haviland; J. F. Faure, sale, 1902, no.38; Durand-Ruel to H. Walters, 1909/10, for $25,000

Selected Reference: For discussion and listing of exhibitions and bibliography, see W. R. Johnston, *The Nineteenth Century Paintings in the Walters Art Gallery* (Baltimore, 1982), 136–37, no.153.

——————————————— *W. R. J.*

JEAN-LOUIS ANDRÉ THÉODORE GÉRICAULT
French, 1791–1824
166 *Riderless Racers at Rome* (1817)
Oil on paper mounted on fabric
17 ^{9}/₁₆ x 23 ^{5}/₈ inches
The Walters Art Gallery (37.189)

In February 1817, Géricault witnessed the race of the riderless Barbary horses that was traditionally part of the celebration of the Carnival of Rome. An ardent equestrian, Géricault was moved by the event to begin work on a monumental picture recording it. Though this project was never realized, more than twenty oil sketches were prepared, including this example, his most literal record of the race.

Provenance: Acquired by Henry Walters at the H. S. Henry Sale, New York, 1907, no.21, for $3,000

Selected Reference: For discussion and listing of exhibitions and bibliography, see W. R. Johnston, *The Nineteenth Century Paintings in the Walters Art Gallery* (Baltimore, 1982), 40–41, no.9.

——————————————— *W. R. J.*

167

168

169

168 PARASOL HANDLE

Russian, Firm of Carl Fabergé (St. Petersburg), c.1900
Workmaster: Michael Perchin (1860–1903)
Onyx, guilloché enamel, brilliants, pearls (original hollywood box)
Height: 2 inches
The Walters Art Gallery (57.1862), Gift of Mrs. Frederick B. Adams, 1956

Henry Walters and members of his family visited St. Petersburg on the steam-yacht, "Narada," in 1900. Walters was introduced to the firm of Fabergé by the American-born Princess Cantacuzene and purchased several bibelots for his nieces, including this parasol handle.

Marks: Michael Perchin and state assay

———————————————— *W.R.J.*

169 IMPERIAL EASTER EGG

Russian, Firm of Carl Fabergé (St. Petersburg), c.1902
Workmaster: Michael Perchin (1860–1903)
Gold, enameled, set with diamonds and pearls
Height: 5 inches
The Walters Art Gallery (44.500)

This egg is believed to have been presented by Czar Nicholas II to his mother, the dowager czarina, Maria Feodorovna, on Easter morning, 1902, in compliance with a tradition that Nicholas' father, Alexander III, had established in 1884. The egg opens to reveal a model in *quatrecouleur* gold of the Gatchina Palace, Maria Feodorovna's residence outside Leningrad.

Marks: Michael Perchin, Fabergé firm, and state assay

Provenance: Acquired by Henry Walters from Alexandre Polovtstoff, Paris, 1930

Selected Reference: Kenneth Snowman, *Carl Fabergé* (London, 1979), 101

———————————————— *W.R.J.*

170 ORNAMENT IN FORM OF A DOUBLE-HEADED FIGURE

Pre-Columbian (Panama, Chiriqui), A.D. 5th–12th century
Gold, repoussé relief
Length: 7 ¼ inches
The Walters Art Gallery (57.262)

Metallurgy developed as early as 300 B.C. in the Andes region of South America. Panned gold was hammered, embossed, engraved and, eventually, cast in a lost-wax technique.

Endeavoring to form an all-encompassing collection, Henry Walters purchased a number of pre-Columbian ornaments from Tiffany & Company, New York, in 1910. According to George Kunz, Tiffany's eminent gem expert, these ornaments had been found by Indians in a graveyard situated midway between Divalá, Panama, and the Costa Rican border during the spring of 1910.

Provenance: Tiffany & Co., New York, 14 December 1910

———————————————— *W.R.J.*

171 ORNAMENT IN FORM OF A FROG

Pre-Columbian (Panama, Chiriqui), A.D. 1000–1500
Red gold, cast
Height: 4 ⅝ inches
The Walters Art Gallery (57.299)

Snakes issue from the mouth of the frog. His large eyes contain copper eyeballs.

Provenance: Purchased by Henry Walters from Tiffany & Co., New York, December 1911

170

17